Hey Amy! I'm a Black Lesbian Rabbi!!!
"and other spiritual insights..."

Rhayne Marcella Thomas

iUniverse, Inc.
Bloomington

Hey Amy! I'm a Black Lesbian Rabbi!!!
"and other spiritual insights..."

iUniverse books may be ordered through booksellers or by contacting:

iUniverse
1663 Liberty Drive
Bloomington, IN 47403
www.iuniverse.com
1-800-Authors (1-800-288-4677)

ISBN: 978-1-4620-2088-1 (sc)
ISBN: 978-1-4620-2089-8 (e)

Printed in the United States of America

iUniverse rev. date: 05/22/2011

Also by Rhayne Marcella Thomas

Gracie-Isms

"I'm 40! I'm Feisty! And there's a gray hair
in my WHAT?!?"

Born Again Bag Lady

Hey Amy! I'm a Black Lesbian Rabbi!!!
"and other spiritual insights!"

I bet when you saw this book you thought, "**What in the ???**" and because your curiosity wouldn't let you live without knowing what was inside, here you are reading it. So Rhayne, what kind of crazy thoughts have you put on paper this time to get us laughing? Well, girls and boys, this time it is about finding yourself but in your own way, through your own journey and from your own perspective. What??? Let me make it easier.

Ever since I was a little girl I realized people didn't know the difference between religion and Spirituality so they lumped them together. Maybe that wasn't a bad idea but it allowed people to keep the age old fight about religion going but with new components. The title of this book just says that if I wanted to be a Black Lesbian Rabbi then I could achieve anything if I wanted it badly enough…and so can you.

Just so you know and before you start sending me emails about how I'm challenging whatever it is that you believe in, let me tell you what this book is not. It is not a manual for finding a religion. It is not a "how to" guide on religion. It is not full of "if you try this…" then life will be better guides. It is also not a reference book to dissect, misrepresent, misuse, disrespect, demean, belittle and/or challenge anything that you do or don't believe in. If, after reading this, you do feel that way then you have missed my message and my blessing.

Most importantly, this is not meant to show you how easy my life has been because it hasn't; and if you can understand that I haven't ever had it easy but I'm still forging ahead and loving life then maybe you, too, can find some relief. And just for the record, *it definitely is not* a story to make you walk up to me and tell me how sorry you are for the things that have happened in my life.

Now let me tell you what this little jewel is. It is a collection of stories (like all my works) that are intended to bless, heal, educate, enlighten and stimulate thinking through laughter and tears, the all natural medicines of life. It is also a way to see that each of us can recreate ourselves if we could only figure out what is needed and where to start. These stories are my interpretation of Spirituality based on how I found it and where you, too, might look for it if you so desire. As always, GOD Bless & Safe Keeping!

To My Wonderful Husband

* For loving me unconditionally when I didn't even know what that meant.

* For not only weathering the storms but, for ALWAYS standing in them with me & holding my hand until they passed.

* For peeling all the layers of pain off my terribly broken heart & mending it together without EVER judging who I was.

But most of all...

* For allowing me to be who you ALWAYS thought I was...a songbird of life.

Thank you for giving me the freedom to find my voice, my passion & myself. I love you very, very much Pumpkin.

(PS: Did I mention you're really cute, too?)

The price of being oneself
is so high and involves so much…

May Sarton

some days you need whiskey
and some days you need w(h)ine.

some days you need neither.

most days you need both...
and I don't even drink!

rhayne marcella thomas

I want to open this page by giving you a little bit of personal information which is unusual because my first name should have been **Discretion** (people who know me are on the floor laughing right now). First and foremost, I don't want you to feel any pressure when you see the word GOD in some of my stories. GOD happens to be who and what I believe in but please feel free to use whatever word you would like over it if you feel the need to do so. Remember, this book isn't about beating religion into you, it's about helping you free yourself from yourself.

Throughout this jewel I will compare and contrast people and animals. Animals, to me, have the ultimate spiritual foundation and if we just watch them we might learn a few things. I will also include insects, natural products and natural occurrences to make a point and/or description more visual and more mentally comprehensible. You have to make yourself remember that this isn't so you can live vicariously through me. It is so you can see yourself living more vicariously through **you**. With that being said, please, please, please take as much time as you need to read this book. I am saying this because there is a lot of heavy duty information and I want you to digest every morsel. Think of it as your favorite foods...you really enjoy them as long as you don't eat too much too soon.

As always, we will laugh, cry, scrutinize and travel with me through my journey and then when the story is over, you will know that it is time for you to get your own bags packed. My journey will not end until life has decided that I'm too much of a one woman party and sends me to Heaven to liven things up. And when it does end, I want to have touched so many lives that when I arrive a Conga line will be in session.

"So Rhayne, why a tale of Spirituality?" asked the donkey." Hmmm...because I don't think I understand religion." Um, okay. Before we go into my personal religion issues, I must say that I will also be referring to family and friends by their names so I have created a page or so of intros and descriptions, so if you forget, you can flip back and get an idea as to why that person was chosen. Those of you who have read my other books will be familiar with many of the names but a refresher course is always a good thing. So let's get to the party!!!

Who *ARE* these people?

My family, (all of my friends are referred to as that) are an eclectic mix of styles, personalities, nationalities, backgrounds and whatever else you can think of. The beauty is that each one has given me a special part of themselves that has enriched my life and made it far more exciting, if there could ever be such a thing. For you to have this gift, you must be open to letting new and unfamiliar people into your life. Not just any people. People that make you feel good in the pit of your stomach upon meeting them. If you've never had that happen, now is the time to hone your skills and become attuned to what your gut tells you so you aren't exposing yourself to danger. Rhayne, you sound like a people expert. Based on my background, I am.

I grew up in The Bronx, New York and my dad was extremely streetwise and made it mandatory from the time I could talk that I would be as well. He made it very clear that if I could sum up any person within thirty seconds, I would never have to worry about being a victim or prey; and he was right. The few times I found myself in a precarious situation it was because I let my guard down and ignored my gut. So, as a rule, I followed the thirty second sum up and kept clear of people who might cause me danger or discomfort. The only problem is, once you stick to this as a written in stone rule, you sometimes miss people who could make your life even richer. It's a learned skill and, as you grow, if you follow your gut, you will figure out who's real and who's toxic. With all that being said, let me introduce you to my life changers.

Pumpkin: My husband of many years. Tall, quiet, handsome, kind, objective, smart, hardworking, generous, loner, romantic, non-judgmental, patient, music enthusiast, thinker, appreciates good food, contemporary, sexy, understanding, loves technology, great listener, loves speed, private, chocolate lover, intentionally elusive, knows when to rest, supportive, hates small talk, rational, night owl, observant, keeps me grounded, motorcycle & car enthusiast, desert lover, expensive taste in everything and married to his exact opposite.

Joan: My Canadian diamond. Great sense of humor, laughs from the bottom of her feet, adventurous, beautiful, generous beyond generous, zest for life, silly, empathetic, non-confrontational, innovative, nurturing, spontaneous, humble, patient, night owl, entrepreneur, financially savvy, non judgmental, makes everything fun, sensitive, girly, thinks the whole world's a stage, smart, humanitarian, ultimate cheerleader, prayer warrior, loves all things beautiful, motorcycle rider of the world, will try just about anything once, expensive taste in everything and always has that little girl twinkle in her eye.

Steve: My Canadian-Ukrainian gem. Also known as Joan's husband. Serious thinker, observant, generous beyond generous, handsome, hardworking, loves dessert, financially savvy, motorcycle rider of the world, brilliant businessman, loves speed when Joan isn't looking, goes to bed at 10pm sharp, smart, appreciates good food, entrepreneur, informative, doesn't take no for an answer, dislikes excuses, a no "cock & bull or shenanigans" kind of guy and enjoys an occasional hootenanny.

Jim T: My Canadian eyeglass specialist. Great sense of humor, good-looking, easy going, nicest guy I've ever met, patient, understanding, hardworking, aims to please, motorcycle rider, generous beyond generous, happy go lucky, kind, animal lover, Blues lover, makes a mean chai tea latte, funny, friend of Steve & Joan and always accommodating.

Moni: My Canadian rival of Bob Vila. Strong, strong willed, hardworking, extremely creative, barn builder, beautiful, generous, tea lover, pottery maker, spice connoisseur, seamstress, multi-faceted artist, yard sale junkie, fantastic cook, animal lover, equestrian, smart, glass maker, quick witted, eye for antiques, great German background, survivor and Jim T's wife.

Ryan: My Canadian Multi Media Man: Also known as my brother and Joan & Steve's son. Sweet, good looking, mega talented, smart, easy going, animal lover, creative, motorcycle rider, multimedia guru, carver of all mediums, animator, fantastic cook, Brussels sprouts king, flavor connoisseur and out of the box thinker.

Tara: My Canadian jewelry designing sister. Beautiful, sexy, shy, kind, generous, creative, focused, sweet, animal lover, strong, strong willed, peaceful, adventurous, loves speed, motorcycle rider, health conscious, strategic thinker, hardworking, great sense of humor, fire dancer, financially conscious and Ryan's wife.

Jim: My Canadian dish breaker. Also friend of Joan & Steve. Kind, handsome, great sense of humor, inquisitive, great conversationalist, interested, exploratory thinker, mild mannered, well traveled and good natured.

Liz: My Canadian dessert queen. Laughs from the bottom of her feet, beautiful, fiery, loves all desserts, vivacious, pointed, candid, great sense of humor, care what may, ultimate survivor and Jim's wife.

Carmen: My friend of 25 plus years. Serious, beautiful, New Yorker, smart, hardworking, focused, driven, kind, extremely generous, loner, not a fan of change, non-risk taker, computer goddess, keeps me grounded, loves technology, private, rational, great listener, loves the ocean, non-confrontational, supportive, intentionally elusive, knows when my stories bend to the left, problem solver, expensive taste in everything, sexy, objective, loyal and extremely dedicated.

Amy: My title's Muse & native Las Vegan. Kind, easy going, ultimate humanitarian, generous beyond generous, nostalgic, great sense of humor, sensual, extremely nurturing, great listener, strong, non judgmental, beautiful, spiritual, analytical, knowledge seeker, awe inspiring, constantly exploring, loves all things, ultimate cheerleader, natural funny bone, prayer warrior, sensitive, evolver, open to getting out of her comfort zones, an anchor, thoughtful, alluring, comforter, objective, loyal and completely trustworthy.

Linda: Another food loving Vegas friend. Energetic, strong, sexy, self made, loves to travel, fitness conscious, financially savvy, fun, beautiful, sophisticated, spontaneous and smart.

John: Linda's husband. Great conversationalist, good decision maker, smart, good with details, enjoys a good meal, fitness conscious, easy going, good sense of humor and good looking.

Florence: My Vegas lunch on the water friend. Shy, smart, great taste in everything, nostalgic, loves old charming homes & places, laughs at my jokes, wine lover, modest, reserved, sexy, observes very well, classy, beautiful, cultured, good sense of humor, kind, non-confrontational, easy going and loves books.

Doug: Florence's hubby: Funny, loves golf, great conversationalist, smart, easy going, social, handsome, open to new things, enjoys life, stands for what he believes, loves books and has a great sense of humor.

Bernie: My Virginia grown woman. Silly, innovative, beautiful, great with money, loves to travel, embraces getting older, knows how to live off the land, food conscious, easy going, sensual, loves to dance, loves the theatre, artistic, functions on 3 hours of sleep, fought for rights during segregation, not easily provoked, peaceful warrior, knows who she is, enjoys a good laugh, enjoys a hootenanny, selective about her friends and knows a bargain.

Kim: My Southern Belle. Kind, religious, spiritual, innovative, ultimate survivor, wants what's best for everybody, brings an inner light into a room, beautiful, embraces everyone, sensitive, funny, contagious and keeps Sweet Tea alive.

Mark & Kali: Kim's Hubby & their Daughter. Mark is calm, intellectual, strong, great conversationalist and keeps funny jokes alive via internet. Kali is one of the sweetest and most respectful young women I've ever known and she is a great example of a young person who loves life, her parents, others and will contribute great things to this life.

Alix: My Arizona "no limits" friend. Funny, innovative, free spirited, yard sale junkie, generous, thoughtful, creative, dances to her own beat, spontaneous, unafraid, great sense of humor, loves new ideas, zest for life, spiritual, riveting, beautiful, adventurous, trend setter, cutting edge, uninhibited, sexy, experimental, loves food, ultimate cheerleader, optimistic, loves a challenge, culturally diverse, imaginative, makes everything fun, ambitious, laughs from the bottom of her feet, socially conscious, eclectic, laid back, accepting and fights for what she believes in.

Anita: My Puerto Rican Rock. Friend of 30 plus years, strong, dedicated, loyal, fighter, strong willed, generous, determined, pulse keeper, New Yorker, knows a crock when she hears it, beautiful, not easily fooled, no nonsense taker, straight to the point, proud, bilingual, optimistic, hardworking, nurturing and real.

Rhayne: Me. New Yorker, music enthusiast, straight to the point, creative, beautiful, strong, determined, spiritual, silly, everything turns to fun, spontaneous, innovative, food lover & enthusiast, experimental, great sense of humor, uninhibited, not easily fooled, adventurous, yard sale junkie, nostalgic, colorful, attracts the unusual, hardworking, culturally savvy, humanitarian, animal lover, imaginative, night owl, unafraid, knows a crock when I hear it, generous, strong willed, out of the box thinker, seamstress, caster, welder, writer, singer, well traveled, avid reader, free spirited, enjoys a hootenanny, loves the winter, loves the ocean, loves to walk, thinks the whole world's a stage and comfortable in all arenas, situations and places.

After reading the characteristics that each one of us has, I'm sure you noticed all the similarities as well as all the differences. Although most of my family members do not know each other, they all share at least one common trait so when each one meets the other there is a natural fit. You should also have noticed that there are many characteristics that do not match but those are the ones that enhance us as a family. In order to create a whole you, you have to have balance because too much of one thing and not enough of another keeps you from attaining a healthy spirit. Let's talk about that a little later but for right now let's explore Spirituality as I know it.

WHAT IS SPIRITUALITY AND WHY DO I NEED IT?

Spirituality. Can you touch it? Eat it? Feel it? Hear it? See it? Hold it? Immerse yourself in it? Can everybody have it? Will I know when I get it? Can I speak of it freely? Will it change my life? Will it change the lives of those around me? Yes to all of the above. I never really thought about Spirituality, at least not until the last few years when I always felt uptight, tired, anxious, depressed, angry and/or defeated; and those were not normal feelings for a fun girl like me. Of course I received hundreds of reasons from everybody as to why I was feeling this way. People mentioned lack of sleep, too much sleep, too much time away from home, lacking vitamins, need a dog, need a church, anemia, you name it. Thank goodness I am someone who is usually in touch with my inner self so a great deal of those suggestions went undone. I had this feeling that something was missing in my soul but it was a hard to describe kind of feeling. A feeling that said I wasn't giving myself something I really needed. In order to do this I had to remove myself from several places.

No matter where I have ever lived or traveled, I have found a way to completely immerse myself in the place itself. I knew where every café, creative class, music jam, poetry night, food tasting, art showing and any other event was taking place. My weekends were filled to the gullet with yard sales, thrift stores, lunches, film fests, book festivals, farmer's markets and drives to nearby towns. For someone like me who gets bored after twelve seconds of not moving, those things were the highlights of my days. Then, at the end of 2002, I moved for the millionth time but to a place that was unlike any other place I had ever been. Since I am the consummate thrill finder, I was, as always, ready to find all those hidden gems. After a few years, I started to slip into a dark place I didn't recognize and that's when I knew I was missing that "something" I couldn't describe.

What does that have to do with Spirituality, Rhayne? Well, it has everything to do with it. You see, all of us have things that make us happy, that allow us to thrive naturally and if we don't get those things we may become a different person. Many times we may not recognize the problem as it isn't always obvious, especially if we've never experienced it before. Our inner Spirit needs to soar and each of us needs to know what it requires in order to feel more alive.

Living in my new place was, and still is, a huge adjustment. I had never been anywhere that didn't offer thrift stores, weekend festivals, cafes, walking neighborhoods, close drives to other towns, museums and/or any of the other pastimes that kept me busy over the years. I never thought about those things contributing to my overall happiness because they were always within reach and I never imagined I would ever be without those things. Although my husband recognized what was happening and expressed it to me, it didn't make it any easier for me because I was still without my natural Spirit fillers and I was going progressively downhill in emotions and lack of stimulation.

Spirituality, for me, is an all encompassing way to nourish the mind, body, soul and heart; **and** fulfillment of **all** leads to balance, wellness and happy living. The one thing I've always been aware of was that most of the people I have met or passed through my lifetime were always just floating through their days. Speaking with people allowed me to see that many were stuck in ruts and situations that seemed hopeless and offered little to no excitement or variation in their present and/or futures. I never understood how someone ended up in those situations when there was so much to see, do, eat and learn. I also learned that many people lived vicariously through me and that was fascinating. Often I tell stories of things I've done or tried and the response is pretty much the same; "I wish I could do that." When I ask why they can't

I get many reasons, such as, "I don't have any money. My husband/wife wouldn't want me to. What will my friends think? I don't want to go alone. What if I catch a disease? What if I don't like it? I wouldn't know where to start." And there are countless other reasons but they all add up to just one thing, and it's a big thing. It's called, **FEAR**.

Fear is the one thing that can stop us from forging ahead. It is SO powerful it even stops us from allowing others to forge ahead. It is also SO powerful it can keep you focused on the past trying to fix things that are long forgotten. I want to spend some time on this subject because if you can get past fear, you can do anything you want.

When I was about seven years old I had a class assignment where our teacher asked us what fear meant to each of us. I can remember writing that fear was something that kept me afraid but probably wasn't real. I am sure I learned this from my dad and his thirty second rule as well as my constant observations of the streets of New York City. New York City is the one place where you can't afford to be afraid of the daily boogeyman because he would know it and seek you out. But, I did have a few real fears such as being on drugs, being an alcoholic, being a mother, being in a committed relationship and being uneducated. For a seven year old those were pretty intense. As a result, I am 44 years old, no children, college graduate, never did drugs or alcohol and my PhD is from the streets of life.

I do have to say that I had another fear that was instilled in me by family which caused great strife. I started singing when I was about 2 years old and people thought I was really good. I sang The Blues as that was my favorite genre of music and I heard it all the time. As I got older more people started telling my parents that they should try to get me on television, radio, etc. because they thought I really had a gift. In eighth grade my chorus teacher called my parents to tell them she recommended I audition for a specialized high school for students who were creative in music and the arts. My parents agreed, I auditioned and I was accepted. Now here is where fear stepped in.

My parents and my other family members made it very clear they didn't think I had any talent and how "entertainment was an impossible career filled with alcoholics and drug addicts." According to them, entertainers became addicts because they couldn't make any money and that was why I needed to go to college to get an education so I could get a "real" job. I was taught that The Bible said, "singing was a vain art and GOD would punish me for being vain." GOD also punishes those who want to be rich because "money is the root of all evil" which was why musicians ended up destitute.

Now you must think back because those were the days when there wasn't any internet, no shows about becoming famous and I didn't know anybody who was rich or famous. Those were also the days where you were taught both at home and in school that whatever your family says is true and they only say those things because they love you. So here I was with a conflict. My spirit was telling me I could make it in the music business but my family was telling me there wasn't any hope. Of course, the more I heard it and the more they came to my performances to tell me how I "wasn't that great" the more fear crept in. It crept in to the point that when I tried to audition for a role I couldn't even open my mouth, thus confirming what I had been told.

My fears became so huge that when I did get a role I would be physically sick for days before a show because I had convinced myself that the audience would see I wasn't talented and I would get booed off stage. The realism of my fears were so grasping that by the time I went to college I stopped singing altogether and I also stopped telling anyone that I could sing. At that point in my life I started trying thousands of different things and none of them made me happy, except singing.

In 1991 I was with my ex-husband who happened to overhear me singing in the car one night and pulled over. He looked at me in pure shock and

I didn't know what was going on because I wasn't aware I had been singing. He said, "I never knew you could sing. You have an AMAZING voice. Why aren't you singing professionally?" I was completely taken aback. I didn't understand why he thought I could sing and even if I could it had been so many years I wouldn't even know where to begin. My response? "Oh. It's not a big deal." His response? Everywhere we went after that he would tell anybody who would listen that I was a phenomenal singer and if they would let me sing for them they wouldn't be sorry. OH NO!!! Fortunately for me most people just kind of waved him off…until one night in a jam packed café while having dinner with friends, the vocalist of the band that was playing said, into the microphone, "I understand there's a young woman here who can really sing. We'd like her to come up and do a tune or two with us!" I couldn't imagine who that could be until she called my name. Can I tell you that I almost died?

First of all, I hadn't performed in front of anyone for over five years and didn't even know if I could remember any of the words to any song I ever knew. Then a really scary thing happened; I could hear the voices of my family telling me that I was getting ready to make a fool of myself again. I was suffocating and my reaction was to run out of that place but there were so many people I couldn't even see the door. Slowly, and I do mean slowly, I looked at the audience who were all clapping and cheering me on, I walked to the stage and introduced myself. Sweat was running down my back, front, down my armpits and into my cowboy boots. My teeth were chattering, my heart was using a sledgehammer against my chest and my ears were ringing. The audience went silent. I turned to the band and said, "Summertime. Key of C. Slow and melodic." Then the intro started. I said a prayer and opened my mouth. When the song was done I received a standing ovation and some dates to come back and do my own gigs with the band! My friends couldn't believe my voice and the thought of doing it again almost killed me but I am someone who gives my word and that is final.

The café performance was in late 1992 and from that point on I was invited to do all sorts of things and each time I had to get a serious hold on myself so I wouldn't need a defibrillator. Shouldn't all of those performances conquer that fear Rhayne? Well, no. As a matter of fact, it started to get worse and I couldn't understand why. In 1993 I met a new friend named Crystal who was funny, beautiful, charismatic and her eyes sparkled like jewels. We somehow got on the subject that I sing and she happened to know that the Braves baseball stadium was auditioning singers for The National Anthem the very next day. I declined.

Crystal showed up the next day, at my job, at 11:00am and took me to the audition with my boss' approval and excitement. I auditioned and they told me I would be singing the anthem for the next three nights and to be there by 6:15pm. Y-I-K-E-S. When I got back to work and told my boss what happened he bought tickets for the entire staff for the next night's game so they could support me. Y-I-K-E-S x 2. Now I was really afraid because my performance was acappella (without music), in a huge stadium and had major feedback. The good news was I would be standing by the dugout (where I auditioned) so no one would really see me. Then it was tomorrow.

By the time I arrived at the stadium at 6:00pm, my head was already beginning to ache, my stomach was sour and the voices in my head were making me feel faint. I went to my post and at 6:15pm the woman who auditioned me came down to the dugout area and said this to me. "Now, at 6:45 the announcer will start welcoming our sponsors. At 6:50 he will start announcing the night's events and then you will hear your name. At that point you will walk out to home plate, turn on your mic and begin." WHAT?!? "I'm sorry, I think I misunderstood you. Don't I sing it from here?" She looked at me as though I just asked her if her daddy wore gartered fishnet stockings. "No honey. Out there. You'll be fine."

And then she was gone. I looked at my watch and it was 6:41. All of a sudden I started to sweat profusely. Then a terrible nausea washed over me. Then I heard the announcer. Then I heard my heart giving my ears an exam. Then I heard my name and saw it go across that humongous board. GOD. PLEASE. DON'T LET ME FAINT. OR VOMIT. My walking felt like I was wearing anvils and I could hear people yelling my name and waving. Before I knew it I was at home plate and there was deafening silence. GOD. PLE-E-A-A-S-E, LET THE VOICES BE WRONG. I opened my mouth, ignored the sound system feedback and then it was over. Cheers and more waves. I walked straight to the dugout, handed that smiling woman my mic, walked up the stairs, out of the stadium, to my car, into my home and collapsed into bed, sweaty to the core.

When I finally woke up there were many messages on the voicemail asking what happened to me and where did I go. Back to bed because tomorrow I have to do it again. Yes it was exactly the same feeling. Many years have gone by since then and many more performances but it wasn't until 1996 when I met my current husband that things really changed. Brian came along and, although it was not a short or easy task, made me believe in myself. He also helped me challenge the fearful voices in my head and kept being my cheerleader. The real turnaround came in 2001 when I wanted to audition for a summer theatre role in Dreamgirls but knew that I would be devastated if I messed up. Brian said, "Babe, you are just as talented if not more than those other people who will be there. I think you should do it." So I went on a rainy night to a place filled with other talented people. I took my portable stereo, audition CD and when they called my name I belted out St. Louis Blues. Then I left.

The next day someone called to ask if I could come back for a second audition. Great. But I went. I went because my husband believed in me and I didn't want to let him down. There were many performers there from the previous night so I sat down and made a couple of friends (yeah, yeah, I know, what else is new?). The director, music director and producer called me and three other young women up and made us stand side by side while they whispered among themselves. Then the music director told me to stand away from the other three. I moved over about four feet and my heart just sank. He told each woman who she would be and handed her a script. I was just standing there. Then he turned to me and said, "You will be Effie White." The lead? That can't be because I can remember when I was twelve years old going to Broadway to see the show and how amazing Jennifer Holiday was, and now I was getting her role? He then asked, "Are you not happy with that role?" I just laughed and so did everyone else.

Once I got home Pumpkin was still at work but called to ask how it went and I told him. He wasn't surprised and told me I was going to be great. And great I was. I put everything I had into those four weeks of rehearsals and was off script by day five. By the time opening night came I was ready. Matter of fact, I was so ready that I wasn't, for the first time in my life, even a little nervous. I received rave reviews from critics and my husband was right there cheering me on as well as friends and strangers. Every night many people brought me flowers and came backstage to tell me how they laughed and cried or how I made them want to perform. Then it hit me. Finally, I was blessing others with my gift. BUT, if this was a gift why did GOD want to punish me for having it? I will address that in the next chapter but let me continue with fear.

FEAR. The acronym? **F**raudulent **E**ditorials **A**cting **R**eal. Notice I said ***Acting***. Meaning pretending or playing a role of something else. Fear grips us when we allow our thoughts to go ahead of being rational. How many times have you dreaded something that still hasn't happened? Or, how many times have you avoided something or someone because you feared the worst? What happened? Just like in my many performances I was so worked up by my thoughts, past and present, I could actually make myself physically ill. My thoughts made a situation that hadn't happened into a catastrophe before I even had a chance to get involved. My thoughts took my power and turned it against me for the worse. On the flip side, if my thoughts could do that couldn't they also turn things for the better for me? If I could maintain a little control, couldn't I get my thoughts to turn fraudulent editorials acting real into positive images?

I must also tell you that when FEAR enters your mind it brings company. Company like: **CHAOS-C**hance **H**appenings **A**cting **O**utta **S**orts and **DOUBT-D**elusional **O**bstacles **U**nraveled **B**y **T**houghts. Chaos and doubt, like fear, are true to their acronyms. Can you think of times when you've raced hundreds of disconcerting thoughts and ideas through your mind and then when your day isn't going well you contribute it to knowing so? What about the possibility that it was a chance happening but because *you* were acting outta sorts it fit right into your previous thoughts? And how about doubt? If fear doesn't get you then it allows doubt to come in and make you second guess yourself so that panic can get in. Doubt takes things that you may know for a fact and creates delusional obstacles in your mind as to why you can't do, go, see and get.

All of us know that once we create a stopping block in our minds it might as well be real because we cannot see our way clear to our goals. Think about what I said when I had to sing. In my mind I had already sung the wrong words, sung off key, fainted, gotten sick and whatever else. And you know what? Many times those exact things did happen because the doubt and fear that I created in my head gave way to an internal chaos that completely immobilized me and kept me from doing the things I knew I could do with ease. It was a form of self-sabotaging and self-loathing. Rhayne, that all sounds good but how do I keep those thoughts out of my mind? Glad you asked.

PEACE. **P**ersons **E**nduring **A**ll **C**hanges **E**asily. Peace is the door that allowed me to start working my way towards Spirituality. My background was one of extreme family chaos, dysfunction and disorder and as a result I didn't know what peace was or how one received it. I had always heard that if I read The Bible I would get peace but that didn't work for me. I was also told that peace came only if you were a good person. Or a Christian. Or a man. Or had children. Peace didn't come to the rich. Peace didn't come to the vain. Peace didn't come to those who made mistakes in the past. With so many conflicting ways to get or not get peace, I became a mental mess.

Looking back I realize I could not have had a healthy relationship because I could not clear my mind of the voices. Voices of fear, doubt and utter chaos. And because I could not settle my mind, I had a knack for making others crazy. I could not keep still. I could not sleep. Anger always took precedence over calm because that was what I was used to and I didn't know there was an alternative. Many have tried to bring me comfort but they just became entangled in my lost world and then hurt. In my heart I **never** wanted to hurt anyone but I didn't know what else to do. I moved constantly to get away from myself but when I arrived at my new destination, there I was waiting for me. That only intensified my anger and fears and made me even more unsure around those I cared about. When you are taught to always be unsure of yourself and to not be vain, you can't make room to love someone else.

Outside of being mentally traumatized and unintentionally mean, I was okay as a person. I have always lived with reckless abandonment because, in my mind, as long as I didn't get in a committed relationship or have kids I was fine. As a result I dodged nice guys and long term relationships. It wasn't that I did not want to get involved, I was always told that "all men cheat" and "all men cheat especially when you are pregnant." My only examples growing up confirmed those statements so I stayed clear. Then I got married. Then I screwed it up royally because I went in with those "man facts" and my own abrasive behavior. My family "knew" I would screw it up and told me so since it was "in my nature to mess up a good thing." How many times had I heard that? Hmmm. Shortly after my divorce, I met Brian and history starting repeating itself, but with one difference; he was willing to take me head on and conquer my fears with me, all in the name of love.

Please believe me when I tell you that there were some tumultuous times but he stood by me and NEVER judged me or what I thought. Brian lovingly guided me to a place where I had never been or even knew existed and, as a result, I started to see things with more clarity. Clarity then allowed me to explore what was real and what was mental. While working through this time I realized some very important truths about fear, doubt and chaos. Fear takes your power from you. Doubt keeps you from fighting before you even get in the ring. Fear and doubt come in many forms and you have to ALWAYS be on guard because together, they create chaos which clouds your judgment. And…I have to add that when I started soul searching I realized fear had a couple more acronyms that made complete and total sense. **F**orgo **E**verything **A**nd **R**un or **F**ace **E**verything **A**nd **R**ecuperate. Just so you know that my journey hasn't been a cakewalk, I am going to tell you about the first one in semi-graphic Rhayne detail.

Forgo everything and run was my theme song even though I did not know it at the times of making my getaway. As a child I had already decided that the first chance I got I would get out of the house and get as far away from my family as I possibly could. By age eighteen I was on the move. I chose a college about eight hours away and although I was in another state, my family kept the insanity going by phone, mail and, when possible, by visitations. As a result I began to flunk all my classes which was extremely disturbing because I had always been an A+ student. Well after one year I decided I wasn't in a good place so I moved again. As a matter of fact, I moved every year to a different place but one thing always stayed constant. The fears in my head never left and were intensified with each move because I could not get grounded. Of course I had absolutely no idea that I was not grounded, but I did know that I was drowning in a barrage of self-doubt, sadness, loneliness and mental anguish that would not go away no matter where I went.

There was one thing that did occur to me and that was, as long as I was busy the "voices" went away. Problem solved. I just stayed busy. All day. All night. All the time to the point of exhaustion and then I would not go to bed until I knew I would go instantly to sleep so the voices wouldn't get a chance to work on me. By the time I was thirty I had moved eighteen or nineteen times and there still wasn't any peace to be had. And you know what was even worse? The voices were getting more powerful, more cruel and more real until I could not decipher if they were telling me truth or I was going crazy. Then I met Brian.

Brian was instantly good for me even though I wasn't so great for him. Here was this handsome man who loved me fearlessly, enjoyed getting a good night's rest, believed in stability, honesty, came from a loving family and had a great moral compass. And then there was me. Intimidated by my past, as I always felt when I encountered a nice guy, told him I was "damaged goods" and "my family was crazy" and that was the extent of information. He didn't pry but the closer he tried to get, the faster I tried to run from the voices so he wouldn't hear them. I know you are wondering why I just didn't tell him the truth. Well, when you start believing the voices it is impossible to explain why you feel the things you do because you don't want someone to think you are a nut. In my case I was certain that if he knew the truth he would disappear and it all seemed too exhausting to figure out how I even arrived at those conclusions. But Brian kept loving me and I kept resisting love. Then one day, many years later, my dad came to live with us and the journey to my mental freedom finally started making sense to Brian.

FEAR. PART II.

Fear plus doubt equals chaos. Or, chaos creates doubt and then fear comes in to help orchestrate more chaos. No matter how you look at these statements the conclusion is the same. Be VERY, VERY, VERY careful of Fraudulent Editorials Acting Real.

Many years ago I stopped wearing a watch. I had taken a college class that was quite liberal and made you think about all issues all the time. My professor asked us to think about time and if we thought we were rushing it or forcing it by constantly checking our watches. She also wanted to know if we didn't wear a watch would we be less timely. On that day I wanted to see if there was any truth to what she was asking so I took my watch off and never wore one again. You know what happened? Nothing other than I felt less pressed to get everywhere and things that used to drag by no longer did. Funny how one small thing like that can change a perception.

Remember in the last chapter how I told you to guard yourself against doubt, chaos and fear? While soul searching I started thinking about my environment and the effects it might be having on me. I also started looking at my family, friends and values. Hmmm. Thinking back made me recall my decision in 1984 to no longer watch the news or read a newspaper since the majority of the stories created anxiety for me. Stories about war, murder, hunger, hatred, unemployment and so on kept me in a state of constant unrest and just reinforced my dad's thirty second sum up rule. Once I stopped getting involved in the truth known as news, I was far more comfortable doing my daily errands. What else had I been spoon fed that kept me from becoming a better me?

Painfully and carefully, I began to look at my parent's and family's views and beliefs that were instilled in me as a child. If I could be taught not to like myself, couldn't there be other reasons why I am not functioning well as an adult? How about the "all men cheat" statement? How about GOD considers my gift of song as vain? After coming up with thousands of "facts" from them over the years I realized that fear can be instilled in you by people, even people who love you, if you aren't careful. And this is where my dad coming to live with us sheds light for my husband.

My dad has always been the same person, before I even came along, and I know this because I have heard many people say so. Without dragging all the dirt out of the pit, he loves the ability to break a person's self-confidence. He was so good at it that I considered it a highly sophisticated art form. He was funny, smart, charming, charismatic, educated, hardworking, extremely social and well liked upon initial meeting. He was also a mean, bitter, egotistical, controlling, argumentative, chauvinistic man who would fight at the drop of a hat and believed all women lived to worship him. My mom was nice, giving, non-confrontational and a people pleaser. She was also a non-maternal, uneducated woman who believed that a man was the key to being alive. To make matters worse, most of the people in their circles were pretty much like them. I don't say these things to disrespect them but only to paint a vivid picture of their personalities and where I fit in.

I was smart, determined, a social butterfly, charismatic, creative, talented, educated, hardworking, kind, spontaneous, giving, funny and full of life. I was also a product of my environment and eventually I learned to become verbally mean, confrontational, sarcastic, a fighter, a girl who wouldn't need a man, a girl who wasn't going to take any crap and a girl who picked up these characteristics all in the name of survival. The problem was I didn't know I had become those things and when I ran into the world, I was ready for all fights. All except the ones in my head.

Remember when I told you to be very careful of the fraudulent editorials acting real? Once my dad moved in my husband noticed my instant change in personality which was me being on guard as I was all the time anyway. Thank GOD Brian is someone who observes a situation very closely before coming to any conclusions. He watched each day as my dad would say things that he considered funny but he knew they were mean and ugly and meant to hurt. He knew because he had been told thousands of times over years and years about the things he says but he says them anyway because he doesn't care how they affect others. But Brian cared and after watching countless ugly exchanges, he came to me and told me he now understood why I acted the way I did all those years and that it wasn't my fault. It had to be my fault because the voices said so. I was a wreck and I knew that if I didn't do something quick I was going to ruin another marriage and continue to be a failure as per the voices. I fell completely apart and a friend of mine sent me to a minister to get myself on the right track, save my marriage, save my mind and free my head of the voices.

The minister wasn't an ordinary minister. He believed in GOD, The Bible and church but he didn't believe in "brow beating you with The Bible." He believed religion should be a Spiritual concept and no matter what you believed in the foundation should be the same. TREAT ALL AS YOU WOULD LIKE TO BE TREATED. I knew that because I had heard it my whole life and that was what I tried to do. He also told me that in order to start my new journey I would have to pray and meditate for GOD (or whomever I believed in) to "Bless Brian and change me." Over the course of three months I would speak to this minister and go to his sermons which always left me feeling like a new soul. Whenever I wanted to get angry or take out my frustrations on my husband I would say, "Bless him. Change me." I took those months to prove I was a good person with good intentions but we all know that after years of violent outbursts I had a lot of work to do.

First things first, I moved my dad into his own place so I would stop being under attack and have the time and focus I needed to dedicate my life to my new path. Let me tell you gang, whoever said "that in order to be built up we must first be broken down" was a genius of internal work. I was at my lowest and I thought I would die from all the pain, guilt, emotional baggage and toxic characteristics I had inside. I cried for weeks on end and Brian was there watching and waiting and reassuring me that I was a good person and none of it was my fault. "Bless him. Change me. Please. Before I die of a broken heart."

The emotions I experienced were unlike anything I could have imagined. There were surges and swells of blame, anger, depression, hatred, despair and hopelessness. I never stopped fighting because I knew that the odds were against me and I was determined not to let the voices be right again. Then one day I woke up and things looked a little brighter. I wasn't as angry. Or venomous. Or unhappy. Or alone. Brian had stood by, and I'm sure reluctantly, as tsunami Rhayne passed. We were looking better and life was starting to return to that fun place that I used to know. And, even though the voices were still there, they started to make sense, and once they did, I had a lot of questions that needed answers so I could move forward.

FEAR. PART III. THE END.
THE BEGINNING.

The last acronym I had for fear was Face Everything And Recuperate. Was that even possible and if it was, where would I start? I started with more prayer, more meditation and more truth. As the voices did all they could to try and drag me back to that black abyss, I would discuss each editorial with my husband. Once I started saying those things the voices said out loud, I began to understand where they came from and that would be the road to recuperation. So where did they come from?

I told you a few pages ago to be careful what you believe and I really meant it. Fear is and can be created through many places. When we are small we may be taught to fear the boogeyman. As we grow older we may be taught to fear other things without knowing why. We may also be taught to fear ourselves and the gifts we have to offer others. You see, I have always tried to steer my thinking in a positive direction so I would get positive results. I believed if I did the right things I would be rewarded and life was this great big thing to enjoy. So where did these voices of doubt come from? They came from people. My family's opinions to be exact and, according to them, they were "doing what was necessary to help me be a better person."

So I started thinking back to childhood. I began to remember all the times someone would tell me how I wouldn't make it as a singer because there were many more talented people out there. Or how I was too fat to be onstage. Or not smart enough to remember any lyrics. As I attacked those "facts" many more started to surface. I wasn't pretty and no man would ever want me. How I would never have any money. How I would end up pregnant and single. Hmmm. Clearer it was becoming. I realized that the "experts" had to find a way to attack the things that might have been sensitive to me because I was hard to scare. I also became aware that they were unhappy vultures who envied my zest for life and did all they could to take it away from me. They also knew that as a child I was on a true spiritual journey to greatness and they couldn't allow that to happen so they attacked me where I was most vulnerable. And it worked because I did not have anyone I could go to for guidance in the opposite direction.

While continually opening up to Brian I found out that he was right. It wasn't my fault but that didn't change all the pain I had caused others over the years so I prayed for forgiveness. I prayed for guidance and for the life I always wanted be restored to me so I can be a blessing to others. I always prayed that prayer as a child so it felt familiar. I prayed constantly for perseverance, change, happiness, wisdom, restoration and forgiveness. Forgiveness was easy. Forgetting was not but I am a work in progress. It can be hard to forget when you are always reminded of the days you lost, and that is why you must guard your eyes, ears and mouth at all times.

My mom used to say, "believe half of what you see and none of what you hear." Truer words have never been spoken. My personal experiences confirmed my beliefs of, "that which creates chaos, fear and doubt will not allow room for peace, faith or order." My family and their friends would thrive on chaos. They loved when folks were arguing, fighting, lying, stealing, cheating and gossiping. I had always hated those things so much that I created a wall between myself and them and that was when the verbal bashings of "how I thought I was better than them" started. Wow. I get it. TREAT ALL AS YOU WOULD LIKE TO BE TREATED. No wonder that now makes sense. They ENJOYED the way they treated others and the way others treated them even though it was not good. Can you see how that statement can work both ways? Once that light came on for me I was able to decipher exactly how I ended up frowning upon religion. Shall we?

Now that I am in a place which has some peace for me I am able to see where all my guilt came from and how I could turn it around. My family and their friends were all "Baptists and Christians." They knew they were going to heaven and everyone else would not because they were sinners as said per The Bible. Especially me.

So, picture this…Sicily, 1936… oh, wait a minute, that's from my favorite show, The Golden Girls. Let me refocus. Where was I? Yes, me the sinner. As a little girl I was force fed The Bible but only as a means of making me feel guilty for not being a "good child" since I was singing and that was vain. I was told daily how vanity was a sin and GOD would punish me for being vain. Here were some of the biggies that The Bible supposedly said:

* money is the root of all evil
* you can't have communion if you are a bad child
* tithing 10% goes to the preacher & he uses it to buy cars
* GOD is Black
* women can't be preachers
* do as I say, not as I do
* idle hands are the devil's playground
* rich people aren't happy because they steal
* thou shalt not worship false gods
* Baptist is the only real religion

By the time I was five years old I had a fifth grade reading level so I was put in Sunday school with the seven and eight year olds and that was when I starting questioning those "Bible" quotes. A few times I was scolded for having a fresh mouth and questioning adults and that was why I couldn't have communion. Going to church became an educational expedition for me because I started to see that someone was lying but I kept it to myself and knew that when I got the chance I would change religions and/or read The Bible to see what was really going on.

As I continued through Sunday school I learned that "the LOVE of money is the root of all evil" (1 Timothy 6:10) and not money itself as there were many wealthy people in The Bible. Being bad had absolutely nothing to do with communion and 10 percent for tithing was a necessary giving of thanks for all that has been given unto you. Besides, if everyone knew the preacher was using it to buy cars they never would have given it in the first place, it was just info for gossip and malicious slander. I also found out that when The Bible stated we should not worship false gods it was not referring to owning material things such as houses and cars. It was talking about giving into fear, doubt and depression because those are fake emotions posing as real but wouldn't exist if you had Faith. Now THAT is deep. And as for GOD being Black, I didn't care if He was a Muppet as long as my prayers were being answered.

Many of the comments above were developed to inflict guilt and used to allow those who swore they were "Christians" the ability to bend the Biblical rules. I don't care if you want to be a Christian and bend the rules, just stay consistent. And don't insult my intelligence. I knew that many people who quoted The Bible to me were illiterate so I didn't pay them any attention. Those who could read were doing all the things that The Bible stated were sins and insisting that it depends on the interpretation. Over my lifetime I have come to know that the word "interpretation" allows wiggle room for lying, gossip, deceit, theft and judging of others; all the things I did not stand for and all the things I was always accused of being or doing.

With mental growth comes more clarity and it became clear that what you say about someone else is usually what you are or are doing. Most of the people I encountered that said they were "tried and true Christians" were the ones I watched drink, curse, lie, cheat, gossip, steal and so on. School and Sunday school really opened my eyes when it came to observing behavior and since I loved people, I wanted to do good things such as sing for them, make them laugh and feed the hungry. All the things that went against what I saw and heard by the "Baptist Christians." So at age fourteen, I began religion hopping.

What could be more refreshing than seeking out another religion to prove that people are good and want to do good things? I began by going to a Black Methodist church that was so similar to the Baptist church I left after only a year but in that year I sang in the choir, read to the congregation and became involved with several church activities. Then I started to hear adults say those familiar things about other religions, what so & so was doing, the preacher and the offerings and then I was gone. Gone to the Catholic church.

The Catholic church took some getting used to because I was unfamiliar with mass, communion process, standing and sitting and kneeling. I showed up for many masses in Vietnamese, Latin, Tagalog and Spanish before I learned that there were different programs each week. At least it kept things interesting. I was shocked that people wore regular clothes like pants, jeans, t-shirts because in our Baptist and Methodist churches you wouldn't be caught dead in "street" clothes all because The Bible so called said, "women couldn't wear pants because they would be taking on a man's role." (Where the heck is that in The Bible?) It took no time for me to get used to being in church for one hour as opposed to three or four hours. I loved the peace, serenity, smell of candles and that no one bothered me while I was there. During the week I would go to pray and enjoy the silence. And one time I even went into a confession booth because I thought it was the bathroom. I walked in and some man was behind a beautiful fabric so I asked him what that was and why was he in there. He (the Priest) explained it to me and I gave a confession, asked him where the bathroom was and returned to my pew to further enjoy the silence.

I have been to many churches but some of the Catholic ones are so ornate and gorgeous that I completely miss what the Priest is saying. So many beautiful windows and doors and paintings that it is reminiscent of a museum. I didn't convert to Catholicism but there was still a void I needed to fill so off to the Muslim temple.

Please excuse my ignorance if it isn't called a temple but it was unlike any of the other religions thus far and I was, as usual, fascinated. A schoolmate took me and I had to cover my hair, wear a dress below the knees, take off all my jewelry and told that I would be second to a man. Uh-huh. I sat through that service and whether or not all of that was true (this was umpteen years ago), I didn't go back. Too many rules and the chances of me playing second fiddle to any man was never going to happen. Too many bad memories and too much heated fuel in this girl's furnace to take orders from strangers.

For several years I bounced back and forth from Catholic to Baptist churches until just recently I found a temple in Phoenix that offered peace and Spirituality through Buddhism, Hinduism and Sikhism worship. Buddhism has always peaked my interest as I love the Indian and Japanese cultures. I can recall reading an article many years ago which made a point of saying they were very Spiritual people. Something so powerful was calling me to that temple that I had to go that Thursday night over two years ago and I was glad I did. When I entered that temple something washed over me that left a lump in my throat. I took a two hour Kundalini yoga class that night with a Yogi and I cried the entire class. There were about twenty-five people there and each person was in her or his own place. I do not know what was making me cry nor could not stop it but by the time the class was over I was wiped out but lighter. As I drove to my hotel in that crisp night air, I was smiling and giving thanks for the cleansing of my soul to its deepest depths. Once in the hotel I slept soundly, effortlessly and, for the first time in my life, without any voices.

Upon awakening I was a new person. I couldn't remember the last time I opened my eyes, felt like the world was in my pocket and life was worth living. So now I'm delving deeper into Buddhism, Hinduism and Sikhism, have encountered many friends who were born into these Spiritual backgrounds, are devout practitioners and are happily helping me to understand the foundation.

For me, the temple feels pure and without judgment. Before any of you get your feathers in a ruff, remember I said, FOR ME, it feels pure. But Rhayne, you can't say that because you haven't been to my church or temple or synagogue and it feels pure and…Yes, I can say those things because one has to know when to enjoy something that feels right and when to stop trying to resuscitate road kill. You may be right. I might enjoy your place of worship more but for right now, my spirit roams free in my new found Spiritual area and although I'm always open to new things, this is what is currently working for my personal growth. So that you know, just a couple of weeks ago I attended a chanting, meditation and prayer ceremony at a synagogue in Washington and it was magnificent. The music was simple, the chanting was riveting, the energy was powerful, meditation was uplifting and the Rabbi's messages and prayers were magical. I was there for a little over two hours and I could not imagine any other place better to be at that time. Please do not confuse religion with Spirituality as FOR ME, they are worlds apart.

I want to brush on this point about people and their religious beliefs. Just because something is right for you doesn't mean it is right for me and you DO NOT have the right to force it on me. AND...you definitely DO NOT have the right to force it on me in the name of your favored religion or deity and then make the statement that you "aren't judging me, you just want me to have what is true and/or real." Do you not see the judgment in that statement alone? Every religion believes its religion is the real religion and you have to respect that from other people's points of view. I don't get into discussions about my beliefs or who I believe in because it is not up for discussion. Religion is an age old fight made more volatile by people not being respectful of what others believe and there is no peace in that for me nor is there an answer. FOR ME, I believe that no matter who or what your choice of worship may be, as long as you treat others with divine respect you can be free in your soul and spirit. How can I be a creature born to help others if I do not respect their choices, opinions and decisions? I believe it was the German poet, Goethe, who once said, "Treat people as if they were what they ought to be and you will help them become what they are capable of becoming." Is that not one of the most profound statements ever made?

Definitions according to Webster's Dictionary 1978:

Religion — a belief in a divine or superhuman power or powers to be obeyed and worshipped as the creator(s) and ruler(s) of the universe.

Spiritual — of the spirit or the soul as distinguished from the body or material matters; showing much refinement of thought and feeling.

How many of you remember that game called Telephone? Maybe you called it something else but you were in a room with many other people, the leader whispered something in the first person's ear and they were to whisper it to the next person until everybody in the room had received the message. Can you think back and visualize the results? By the time the third or fourth person got the message it was slightly different and by the time the last person got it, it was totally different than its origin. What do you think happened? I have played that game hundreds of times with people of all ages and the original message never made it around. Perhaps some people couldn't hear. Or, perhaps, and only perhaps, maybe it was each person's interpretation of what was being said, sort of paraphrasing. So what is wrong with paraphrasing Rhayne? Maybe nothing. Let's explore it a little more for the fun of it.

Last year I called a friend and told her that one of my other friends is helping me to understand Buddhism because she is Japanese and lived most of her life in Japan. I also told her that I had been invited to go to Japan to visit her and her family and I am going to do it. About two weeks later I ran into another friend who said, "Hey Girl! I ran into So&So last week and she told me you were going to China and that you were no longer a Baptist because you were going there to study with the Hindus and you know that the Christian Bible is the only truth and their Bible was written by a man and blah, blah, blah…" Hmmm. Anyone who knows me knows what happened next. I called the message giver and I asked her exactly where did she get that information she gave to friend B and she told me that it was what I said. I said, "I never told you that I was going to China. I was going to Japan and I never mentioned anything about The Bible or religious decisions. And what is this mess about studying with the Hindus? And...if I did decide that was what I was going to do, it is NOT up for discussion as it is NOT anyone else's business. Period."

Now here is where interpretation stepped in. She said, and I quote, "Well I knew you were going somewhere in Asia where those people aren't Christians. Besides, what's the difference?" There is a HUGE difference. In her words she was "shortening" the story but assumed the details were the same based on her knowledge, or lack of, Asia, Hinduism, Buddhism and not to mention her total disregard and disrespect for another person's culture and religion. It was not her duty to judge based on what she believed in. Then she added, "Well, I'm not judging you...I just want to make sure you get into Heaven." What comes next is what Joan calls a "Killing a Mosquito with a Bazooka" moment. "Really? Then what exactly would you call it if you weren't judging? Where in The Bible does it say it's your job to get me into Heaven? Instead of worrying about getting me into Heaven, why don't you worry about all that profanity you use Monday through Saturday? Or how you have several kids out of wedlock? Or...how you don't like certain races? Doesn't The Bible discuss those???" Do you know what her reply was? "Well, Rhayne...those aren't as bad as not being a Christian. Besides, GOD forgave me." Wow.

FOR ME...religion's definition leaves too much room for people to take a hard and fast statement and add or take away from it based on their own personal experiences. Think about parenthood. What makes a parent good or bad? Isn't it based on what you know, where you come from and what you are trying to achieve? Yes, some things are seemingly concrete such as a child's punishment or reward but isn't that also based on your background? My personal religious beliefs are exactly the same as I did not like the way my background interpreted religion because it seemed one-sided, used for personal gain and called upon to make an opinion a fact. I also saw it as a way to divide and separate people and I didn't want that. I wanted to know everybody, regardless of what they believed in so I could learn new things. So, in steps Spirituality.

FOR ME…Spirituality's definition works as there are not any rules written in stone. I LOVE the phrase, "showing much refinement (improvement) of thought and feeling." If I can improve my thoughts and feelings, I could make myself a better person and then do what I could to help others if they wanted my help. Notice I said, **if** they wanted my help. My religious background did not give me the option of want because if I thought differently it was a known "fact" that I was going to get the religious help anyway because somewhere in The Bible it said so. Do you have any idea how many times in this life I have been reprimanded, yelled at, sat down, dragged to sermons, read verses and force fed religion as my family and their friends knew it? Do you know how much resistance you get when you try to force something on a child or adult? Because my family had interpreted The Bible based on their needs, backgrounds and what they had been told, it left a terrible taste in my mouth. Many nights I had to sit and listen to someone who decided that as a "real" Christian it was their appointed duty to make me want to be a Christian so I could go to heaven and because I was "straying" I would go to hell.

At age fifteen I had been trapped at the millionth religious gathering in the South where everyone there decided I was a true sinner because I was artistic, creative and a singer…things that did not run in our genetic makeup so it must be from the devil. Having more than enough, I was fuming and sick of it, especially since I was pretty well versed in The Bible by then. After a couple of hours of Bible bashing me, one of my family members told me that I was a sinner and was destined to hell. I looked her straight in the eye and said coolly, "Doesn't The Bible say that ye shall not judge lest ye be judged? And doesn't it also say that you should not bear false witness against thy neighbor?"

She wanted to know exactly what that was supposed to mean so I laid it out in plain, unfiltered terms for her and everyone else there. "Everyone in this room is always talking about someone else and most of the time you aren't telling the truth. All of you go to church every Sunday and then you come home and laugh about who's wearing a raggedy dress or who's husband is cheating or that the preacher is stealing the offerings so he can drive a new Cadillac. Then, during the rest of the week all of you are drinking, stealing, cheating, cursing like sailors and deciding on who is a Christian and who isn't. If all of you are Christians, how do you get to do those things AND go to heaven AND decide who is good enough to join you? How did you come to the conclusion that Baptist is the only real religion? AND, if that is so, I want to see where it says that in The Bible or The Koran or The Vinaya Pitaka?" The result?

First, there was silence. Not the kind of silence that says peace but the kind of silence that might be the opening of a brawl once said information is processed. Remember, I was my dad's daughter so a fight would have been right up my alley. After what seemed like hours, I was rebuked, scorned and told that I was no longer welcome in the church and I wasn't as smart as I thought I was. "Oh, okay...now there is real Christian behavior." And that just added more wood to their fires.

To make a long story longer, everyone starting leaving and telling my mother how I would be the death of her and how GOD would punish me and a bunch of other stuff to which I replied, "That which you say to me will be cast upon you!" Eight ball, corner pocket!!! That was a catch-all that I had heard all of them use in the past when they were the main character in a gossip story. The funny part of that whole situation (yes there is a funny part to me!) was, if they really believed in what they were saying, why did they get so bent out of shape with me? Was it because they knew I was onto something? Or could it have been that they knew I was very well read, could no longer be fooled and I might even pass this knowledge on to others? No matter what, at that point I decided I was pretty much done with religions that decided my fate based on human interpretations. The one thing I have to add though, is that every religion I have studied has given me something new and wonderful. Each religion has its own set of "rules", "truths" and "fanatics" but the bottom line seems to be that all want to be acknowledged with respect, honor, love and to be a vehicle for peace for whatever Higher Power they choose to accept. I have also learned that each religion has its own way of doing things and I respect those things whether or not I believe in them.

It was a very fortunate thing that I was born and raised in New York City as that gave me the chance to interact with many cultures, religions and educational levels. New York City is a plethora of knowledge, with or without consent. There are so many interesting places to go, things to eat, people to see, things to do and not to do. Since I went to school in Manhattan I never missed a chance to be a part of whatever was going on. I found myself at museums, shows, gallery openings, parades, costume diners, hidden restaurants, unusual boutiques, multi-cultural coffee and tea houses and cathedrals. Oh the beauty of the cathedrals will take your breath away!

Due to school trips and projects I eventually found myself at Gregorian chants and Chamber music festivals in those cathedrals. Some of the churches were tiny and some were immense but the feeling was the same; intimate and touching to my soul, to my spirit. And no one seemed to care what my religious background was. I did not know it then but those places had been instrumental to me as a musician and as a person. What I did know was that when I was in those festivals, cafes, parades, etc, I was on top of the world or, feeding my spirit. Those things were who I was and the more I immersed myself, the better I was becoming. Then, by the time I was seventeen I was rushing graduation so I could get "away" from the people who didn't believe in me. Eighteen came, I left and that's when the voices started taking over, removing those things that I so enjoyed and pulling me off of my path.

½ Of What You See. None Of What You Hear.

So far we have explored fear, chaos, doubt, religion, some spirituality and more fear with the conclusion that you must guard your ears, eyes and mouth at all times. I get it Rhayne but where are some of the places those who provide fear may hide? Good question.

Please be aware that not everyone is going to have your best interest at heart or be happy about all of your dreams and accomplishments. Many times it is not intentional to be mean but there are many people who would do anything to do the things I do. So many people tell me how they dream of doing some of the things I have done but, because of a little jealousy, they follow the compliment with a negative comment. I have performed so many places and my books are doing so well but it is only due to hard work, constant marketing and diligent friends who love me. Of course it doesn't stop people from always walking up to me and telling me how they wish they could do what I'm doing BUT…"I know someone who tried it and it failed. My sister did that and she never made a dime. There are so many talented people out there I don't see how you are going to make it. Singers are a dime a dozen. Why do you think your books are special?" and other mindless comments.

Thank GOD for tough skin and a new support system or I would crumble. Those statements are just sidebars from their envy, jealousy and being bitter that they can only dream. Sure singers are a dime a dozen, but doesn't that also apply to lawyers, doctors, carpenters, engineers and architects? No matter what your chosen field may be, how is it that people think you are guaranteed to succeed or fail? What about hard work? Do they really think I just sing or write without busting my humps? Nothing is guaranteed but as long as it stirs your soul and you are happy, who cares? If you have any free time, just do some research and see what successful people say about making it. Most of them commented on how others thought their ideas were stupid, foolish, childish and so on. Joan and Steve have taught me that if I am to become successful, I must surround myself with those who are like-minded.

Be wary of comments which seem innocent because they can deflate you, especially if you have had trying times getting yourself going. I love to travel and I don't care if I go alone as long as I get to go where I want. Guess how many times people say to me that it sounds fun but aren't I afraid of getting raped? Or my car breaking down and someone kidnaps me? Or someone breaking in my hotel room and attacking me? Or my plane crashing? Or being in a tornado? Since I am a true New Yorker, born and raised in The Bronx, riding on subways, none of that stuff bothers me one way or the other. But, what does bother me are people trying to plant those tiny seeds of fear. If you are not strong then those seeds will grow in your mind to the point of paralyzing you from enjoying life.

Do you know that my chances of getting hit by a drunk driver in my car, in my neighborhood, are ninety percent compared to the one percent of my plane crashing? How about the rapists and kidnappers in your neighborhood? If we flip that attitude around how about the millions of folks who travel alone, stay in hotels all over the world and have the time of their lives? Or the singers that you have never seen on the Grammy's that make a fortune traveling the world in unknown bands? Keep your focus. And do not make excuses for people's comments and behavior. "So&So is really nice, I'm sure she didn't mean it that way. Maybe she was just having a bad day." Is that really a cause to say something discouraging to someone else?

On a daily basis I run into people who say that their spouse or parent or best friend is always saying something negative to them and they don't like it. "So why don't you tell them?" "Well, Rhayne, I am sure they didn't mean it…and besides, you know how family can be." As a matter of fact I do and I DO NOT tolerate ill behavior in the name of family or friendship. If someone really cares about you and you have told them multiple times how their comments make you feel and they don't change it, doesn't that tell you something? Perhaps they enjoy hurting you because they are hurting. Perhaps they don't respect you or your ideas. Or, maybe misery just loves company. Are you being fair to yourself to always surround yourself with those who are not like minded? Can you really continue to stay positive in a negative place? We have all been there trying to decide how much time to spend with someone who makes us feel uncomfortable and it is no fun. Nor is it a great way to spend your time as it can deplete your energy and keep you second guessing your potential. If you want to do great things you are going to have to start making harder choices.

Another thing that can be hard to do is being careful WHO you share your joy with. Did you ever have a time where you bought, did or went somewhere special and couldn't wait to tell someone? Can you think of how you thought you would burst if you didn't share it with the first someone you saw? Can you remember how you felt if you told someone and they didn't think it was a big deal or started to criticize? Instant joy killer. I have learned over the years that some things are not meant to be shared with everyone, only those who are like minded. Sometimes there are things you can't tell anyone because they are your own sacred thoughts, ideas and/or places. All of us are aware of times when we were having a magnificent day and then one foul comment or encounter just ruined it. Isn't it funny how quickly one small thing can make you forget how great the bigger things are? So, as a result, I have learned to make sure if I want to share something, it is with others who would be just as excited as I am or I just keep it to myself. Why let one percent erase ninety-nine percent?

Now let's talk about the media. The information passed down to us from the media is enough to make you dig a hole in your wall and live in it. I told you I stopped watching and listening to the news years ago because it was overwhelming but if you enjoy it that is okay, just try to remember that everything you see and hear may be an interpretation of what is really going on. The media loves mass chaos since it can increase ratings, change where we go, what we eat, who we are mad at, what we will and will not support. Good example:

When I lived In Virginia it would snow every winter. Sometimes it was a big snow but most times it was just a few flurries. The first winter I lived there the weather service called for snow flurries on that particular Tuesday in 1992 and for me it was business as usual so I headed for the supermarket after work. Guess what? The market was INSANE! People were everywhere, the lines were twenty people deep and EVERYONE had milk and bread. I had no idea what was going on so I asked one of the line standers. After many intense glares from those within earshot he told me it was going to snow and if we got stuck inside the house there would be milk and bread to tie everyone over. I busted out laughing and went home where I had an endless supply of canned goods, a manual can opener, flashlights with fresh batteries, a shovel and rock salt. I just couldn't imagine what would make all of those sane people rush to buy milk and bread when a storm might have them inside for days.

By the time I got home three flurries had fallen and there were accidents left and right. Once I settled in I clicked on the television and every channel was warning people to "get inside, be prepared for school closings, make sure to have plenty of milk and bread in case it turns into a blizzard" even though the actual prediction was for one inch. The next day I went to work with no snow on the ground and asked my co-workers if that was normal. Everyone said it was a known fact that if the weather called for snow you ran out and grabbed milk and bread. Laughing, I asked, "If there was a blizzard, what good would milk and bread do? Bread would mold and milk would spoil, especially if the electricity went out." It was like a room filled with deer on a dark road when headlights hit their eyes. "What would you buy, Rhayne?" "Um, the same things I bought when I lived in New York. Canned goods, bottled water, a manual can opener, batteries for my flashlight and transistor radio, a shovel, rock salt for my walkway and a window scraper." More road deer. They said that never dawned on them. Fraudulent Editorials Acting Real.

I want to get on with the rest of this book so in closing this chapter here are a few other suggestions where you might want to guard your eyes, ears and mouth.

Keep your thoughts in the present and don't let anyone, including yourself, constantly remind you of past mistakes. We've all made them and wallowing in regret does not allow you to move forward.

Always be alert. If you find yourself constantly trying to explain why you are doing the things you do or getting defensive, that might not be the crowd for you.

Television, radio, newspapers, gossip, hearsay and debates. I'm not saying don't engage forever, just until you have your thoughts in order and are strong enough to recognize when a situation is not good for what you are trying to accomplish.

Advice. You know what? I like that one so much I'm going to give it its own chapter! Follow me ladies and gents.

Whoa. Your chef does your taxes? When I was in junior high school I had an English teacher that I just loved. Mr. Mondorf was his name and he was a great scholar who taught in unconventional ways that made lasting impressions. In eighth grade he told our class that as we get older to be careful where we get advice and only go to experts in the field we needed. He said, "If your chef does your taxes, what are the chances of the IRS having to audit you?" I never forgot that in all these years.

I cannot thank Mr. Mondorf enough for instilling that into my child mind back then because it was easily recognizable as the years went on. The advice I have recognized the most were poor people always giving me advice about money. As a young adult I took their advice because I didn't know any wealthy people and the results have always been the same. A complete mess in my finances. I had people who were in their own financial chaos doing my taxes and then I wondered why I owed the IRS every year. I had lifelong renters giving me advice on real estate and I, too, ended up wanting to buy but knowing I couldn't based on their words of wisdom. Then, when I went to college I met students who were from extremely wealthy families and while listening to them talk, I knew I had been bamboozled by amateurs.

Once I saw the wealthy I knew that was the life for me but I didn't have a clue where to begin. I wasn't comfortable asking them because I had been taught to "know my place" and rubbing elbows with the rich wasn't it. But, I became friends with a few of the students and they talked freely about how I could buy a house, patent an idea, have a CPA for my taxes, travel the world and whatever else I wanted to know. Do you know how ecstatic I was once I had all of this info? But, as we all do before we learn, I tried to share it with the "experts" and they laughed in my face. I was told that "those people" were trying to trick me and that their advice on real estate didn't make any sense and the list went on and on. Although I was sure those wealthy kids were being truthful, I had no way to know so I tried one piece of advice given to me by one of my hall mate's fathers who was a financial guru.

At the time I was getting almost zero financial aid because they said my dad made too much money, which didn't make any sense because we were, by no means, even close to being middle class. I told her dad, he looked over all of my financial aid forms then gave me some other options to inquire by writing because they gave grants. So I wrote to those places and the second semester I received over $5000.00 in money I did not have to repay! My hall mate and I went to lunch a few days later and I asked her how her dad knew I could get that money, to which she replied, "You just have to know where to look." I told the "experts" about my grants and these are the things they had to say. "I bet that money is illegal." "When you buy a house they're gonna garnish your wages for that money." "I bet you had to lie to get it." Now it was beginning to get real clear to me who knew what and who was full of poo-poo. Poo-poo! Hahaha! What a funny word! Side splitter! Oh I just crack me up!!! What? Oh yeah, advice.

After that grant experience I decided to wade a little further into the waters of the wealthy words and hired a CPA. The result? I never owed the IRS again. He knew about deductions, tax laws and all sorts of things that made life much easier for me. I even bought myself a little weekend condo on the ocean in Atlantic City at age twenty-two. There was only one problem for me; once I left school I had to go back to the area I was from which no longer exposed me to wealth. I started making unwise decisions again based on the small amount of knowledge I gained before I left. The only difference this time was, I kept my mouth shut and my choices were solely mine. Since these were the days before the internet, I read everything I got my hands on and spent countless hours at the library trying to piece together my life. Sure I've made some terrible mistakes but I have also made great things happen and my choices were based on what I learned, not what someone told me. My choices were also based on going to the people who were experts in my field of need. Quick, funny story, then we will move on.

A friend of our family, Ms. Jones, had dropped a cast iron frying pan on her foot and broke her foot in several places. After getting much advice from "the experts" she went to a "doctor" that supposedly specialized in broken bones and could "save her money" by not going to those "fancy" doctors at the hospital that just want to "steal your money." After a couple of weeks in a cast Ms. Jones' foot became more painful and her toes were turning black. She went back to the "doctor" and there was a note on the office door telling patients to go to his other office. Her husband drove her to the other address but they kept circling the block because the address she had wasn't for a doctor's office, it was for a rib joint (a little hole in the wall). They finally parked and went in the rib place to see if anyone knew where the office was and, to their horror, there was the "doctor" cooking ribs behind the counter. The address was correct as he had also set up an "office" in the back of the restaurant.

After some choice words she demanded to know what was going on, so he told her. The "doctor", who came highly recommended from some "experts", was a full time cook who always wanted to be a doctor so he opened up a practice on the side. So what's wrong with that Rhayne? Nothing...nothing other than the fact he didn't have a license to practice medicine. She ended up having to go to a "fancy" doctor that she found through a real hospital with her foot having to be rebroken and reset. Now here is the funny part!

When she went back and told the "experts" what happened they told her (are you ready for this?)

they knew he didn't have a license but why spend all that money on a real doctor when you can get the same service and a good meal? Hahahahaha! It doesn't get any better than that! Ms. Jones almost lost her foot for the sake of taking advice from people who had no idea what they were talking about! The morals to this story are: Be careful where you get your advice and make sure you do your research.

Remember this from me: you wouldn't let a shoe cobbler do your hair or a baker fix your car...so don't let just any random person tell you how to fix your life. Find out for yourself. And speaking of finding out for yourself...

Yes I'm An Addict. And It's All Your Fault.

Addict: to give oneself up to some strong habit, according to Webster's New World College Dictionary. There are many different types of addicts; drugs, alcohol, food, spending, hoarding are just a few but there is one in particular that can compromise your journey's decisions if you aren't careful. I call those people, "Drama Addicts."

Drama addicts are dangerous because you may be one, not know it and that is where it can become detrimental to your Spiritual growth. I am sure you remember all the things I said about allowing negative stuff to persuade you but what if you are your negative? The worst thing about people is that we have been so beaten with negative reinforcement that we are skeptical to try and believe positive reinforcement. Sometimes we are so heavily laden with negative information that we wouldn't recognize good data if it were hand delivered. Drama addicts have found a way to make every situation ugly, depressing, gloomy and, most of all, someone else's fault. That's right, the blame shifting game. We are all guilty of it but it becomes problematic when your entire life has become someone else's fault.

It is so sad when you find that drama addict because, if you aren't strong in what you believe, that person can sway your decisions and upset your applecart. That person can also make you constantly second guess yourself even after you are sure. I know everyone has not been given a fair shake at life but in order to find peace, you have to let go of the excuse that whatever is ailing you is someone else's fault. The scariest part of blaming someone else is that most of the time they aren't even aware that you are holding a grudge so they aren't effected in the least by your problem. You, on the other hand, are angry, sad, addicted to who knows what and going through life with a chip on your shoulder, wasting away time that could be used for enjoying yourself. Don't get me wrong, I am certainly not judging because I had to face my own issues to get to where I am today so I know first hand that you have to shake the drama from yourself as well as others.

In my lifetime I have carried anger to the point that it ruined great relationships and potential opportunities, not to mention exploding in situations that weren't explosive. Although I chose not to drink or use drugs, it might as well been the same because it had the same affect on my mind and body. And…it was someone else's fault. And it was but they didn't think so and that just fueled my anger. When I say it was someone else's fault, I am true to the fact that those particular persons molded me in childhood to think a certain way that led to me missing out on things I really wanted to do. When I finally confronted them after many years of anger, they nonchalantly brushed off my accusations. Can you imagine how foaming at the mouth mad I was that they wouldn't even apologize once they knew how I felt? Do you have any idea how long it took for me to realize that now the ball was in my court? I had to figure out how to rid myself of those emotions because as long as I was an anger addict, they would continue to have control over my life and I would continue to miss out on my blessings.

So what did you do Rhayne? What did I do? I'll tell you what I did. I became angry all over again. Every time I thought of how they took zero responsibility for creating the monster voices in my head I wanted to choke them. I would get so worked up that I would break out in a sweat, my neck would be stiff as a board and my teeth would be clenched so tight that I could barely open my mouth. I played that scenario over so often that I would dream about it and wake up sick to my stomach. The drama was feeding the drama and the anger was fanning the fire. It got so bad that I could not stand to be in a room alone because it was the only thing I could think about. And then, other people who were drama driven started appearing in my life and added more fuel to my already hell hot anger. Like truly attracts like. The other addicts would make my sore spots open wounds then pour hot sauce, vinegar and rubbing alcohol in them. Looking back, it is kind of funny that everyone knew how my life was going to play out and in some way, they were correct. If I had continued to feed with them, my life would have continued being just as miserable as theirs and that was exactly what they wanted. Thank GOD for a healthy minded husband and healthy minded friends who wanted me to flourish!

With loving words and loving examples I was taught how to forgive and let go. Yeah, yeah, you've heard that all before and it doesn't work. Oh but it does. But there is a secret to making sure it works. The secret is this: You must keep your mind on positive things as much as possible and not allow others to rope you into old dirt. If someone wants to bring up bad memories, you take control by letting them know you are not interested. Or walk away. Or sever that relationship. Like attracts like. I have watched that my entire life. Watch for yourself. Go to a home improvement store and look in each aisle. People who love flowers aren't in the plumbing section. People who love paints aren't in the lighting aisle. All the people who are gathered in each aisle have something in common. Sometimes you will see total strangers chatting happily about whatever they all gravitate to in that section. Personalities and addictions are no exception.

I have met people who have told me that no matter where they go they meet the "wrong" crowd and somehow end up in trouble. How come others never meet that crowd? I don't run into that crowd because they can tell I have no interest in them or trouble. You have to take matters into your own hands to bring into your life what you need. You MUST, MUST, MUST, this very minute, make a pact with yourself to work on forgiving whomever you are angry with. If your issues have directed you to an addiction that is so powerful you don't know what to do, don't panic. There is help for you but you must want it. YOU MUST WANT IT. REALLY, REALLY WANT IT. You must want it more than you want to stay angry. Or depressed. Or judgmental. Or whatever is trying to hold you down. And I am telling you firsthand that it was tough. I didn't think I was going to make it. It was so much easier being angry. But I did it. And like all addictions, I continue to work at it one day at a time. Some days are definitely better than others but it is okay because I promised myself I would give it my all…and I do. And if you really try, you will win over your addictions and life will start to slowly unravel its goodies for you that are so much better than the addictions.

"I Sure Wish I Was A Snake," Said The Oyster... "I Wish I Hadn't Eaten That Mouse," Said The Snake...

Why, Mr. Oyster, would you wish you were a snake? "Because I wouldn't have this grain of sand irritating me and I could slither across the country and sneak up on my prey and I would be strong and ominous!" Then how would I get a beautiful pearl necklace for my birthday? Or how could I enjoy Oysters Rockerfeller? Or how would I remember my visit to the beach when your fallen shell came home with me as a reminder? "Golly Rhayne. I didn't know I mattered to anyone." Really? Let's ask Senor Snake what he thinks about you wanting to be a snake.

Senor Snake, my friend Mr. Oyster wishes he were a snake instead. "Oh my, that is too bad. I like being a snake although there are some complications. I want to make friends but everyone is afraid of me. Mice won't come near me because once, when I was starving, I had to eat one. I would like to create something of beauty but I don't know how. And, I would love to enter the Strongman competition but I don't have any arms and legs. But it isn't all bad. I tan most days, slither to new locales and enjoy my beautiful skin." "Wow. I never thought you had any problems. But just so you know, you do create something beautiful. Long after you're gone humans wear your colorful skin as bags and boots," said Mr. Oyster. "And you had to eat that mouse. You needed to eat in order to survive so you could continue your species." Rhayne, what on earth are you talking about? Are you sure anger was your only addiction? Yes I am sure.

The point of this story is that you have to be happy with who you are and know that you bring beauty to the world in some form even if you don't see it. Take a good look at yourself and be gentle. Stand in front of a mirror and just look at how you are made.

Are your limbs working? Is your heart beating? Are you healthy? Make a mental list of all the things you are good at because everybody is good at something. Perhaps you are a good parent. A good listener. Good at handling money. Don't get caught up in specifics. Do this exercise everyday until you can find at least three things about yourself that you can polish and offer the world. Take that grain of sand and turn it into a pearl. And while you are working on that sand make sure you keep it in the now. Do not look back.

But I have to look back so I can...I know. So you can continue to badger yourself. Regret has no place in moving forward. Regret can conjure up some of the worst feelings known to mankind. I must tell you that I fight everyday to not long for the past. I have revisited my past so often I can pinpoint the exact day of each mistake and then I beat on myself for making that mistake.

Before I make a decision I pay unnecessary homage to my past mistakes and know that I am never going to make a good decision because history repeats itself. And I am not going to get anywhere because my past reveals I'm not smart enough to keep up with those who have succeeded. The list goes on and on and it keeps me at bay with myself. So I make myself say the opposite each time regret tries to pop in my head. Sometimes it catches me off guard but I am getting good at overriding the thoughts. I tell myself that I am smart, funny, world famous and my past has no bearing on my future. During one of my meditative moments I figured out that my "mistakes" weren't mistakes after all...they were experiences to help me become the person I am today. Those experiences helped me to live a life full of interesting turns and twists that make for good books.

Regret is a woman. What? I have decided that regret is a woman. Who else could dig up something from eighty years ago and make it seem like something that needs to incite a fight today? As a woman, I am a pro at remembering ridiculous stuff from forever ago then bringing it up to my husband who looks at me in a way that lets me know he has no idea what the heck I'm talking about or why that info would matter. I wish I could remember where I put my keys the way I remember what someone said to me in 1983 at the Loews Theatre on Fordham Road in The Bronx. Regret has the same affect.

Sometimes a song will come on from ten years ago and instantly I regret not having made better plans. Or a television show from twenty years ago will come on and I regret how I never had the chance to be on that show. What about arguments? Ever replay those and wish you had said blah blah instead of nah nah? Do men do this? All of my female friends wish they had been better mothers, better career women, better choice makers and other things that do not matter in the present time but sit on our shoulders like mounds of steel. My male friends can't seem to remember anything longer than a few days ago unless it has to do with cars. Hmmm. Must write book about that.

Another trick of regret is to allow other people to make you feel regret. How many people do you know that give their parents, spouses or kids the ability to make them feel guilty for not being there? Or for a divorce? Those life decisions can keep families torn apart for years all because one person becomes the blame and then the dumping ground for everyone else. In order to find peace you will have to decide to forgive the others, forgive yourself, know that you are not responsible for anyone else's long term anger and no one else has the right to hold you prisoner based on decisions you made that you thought were good at the time. Even if you thought they were bad at the time you still made them and life goes on. You ate your mouse for whatever reason was necessary at that moment and you don't have to suffer the rest of your life because you made a choice years ago.

But Rhayne, I made some awful decisions in my life. You don't have any idea how bad a person I was. I can't possibly go on. You can and you will. I did and I made some choices that were less than scrupulous. Looking back I sometimes wonder what I was thinking when I visit my past choices. How could a sane girl like myself come up with such crappy ideas? The beauty of it though is that I had ideas. Every idea I had was all in the name of fun. I wish someone had come along and told me that I needed to get serious about something, and maybe someone did but I was too busy running from myself to get a clear head. I was also too busy feeling guilty about making, what I thought were, bad choices. And maybe they were bad just because they caused me to lose sight of what I really wanted but each choice gave me a valuable lesson for the future.

So remember…be gentle to yourself and allow yourself to forgive a little more each day. Be aware of your emotions and substitute positive words for negative ones. Be proud of small accomplishments because those are the ones that are going to take you where you want to go. Never underestimate a good deed and/or decision no matter how small it may be. And always remember that a tiny grain of sand can be transformed into a valuable jewel with time, patience and persistence…said the oyster.

IF IT'S NOT BREATHING, DOES THAT MEAN IT'S DEAD?

Have you ever watched wildlife or television documentaries on animal behavior? If you have then you are well aware that animals know when the fight is over because they move on to something else. Let's take bees for example.

Bees are busy little insects that buzz from flower to flower, pollinating, tasting each flower and humming a little tune while doing so. A bee will go to a flower, get what it needs and move on to another tasty morsel. Sometimes they will double back on a flower but once they realize it no longer serves their purpose they quickly move along. I can guarantee you have never seen a bee arguing with a flower trying to make it sweeter, juicier or better. And you probably haven't seen a bee on a flower for hours trying to prove a point to the bee kingdom.

How about crocodiles and alligators? When they want to eat they do it with purpose and strategy. They sneak up on their prey, drag them back to their territory and roll them underwater until they are dead. Once that is over they eat, go about their business and rest. Have you ever seen them go to a bunch of bones and start the process all over again? Why would they do that when the prey has served its purpose? Lastly, let's look at the komodo dragons.

Komodo dragons are big, not very fast and may eat everything in sight but most things can avoid them due to their inability to be quick. So what do they do? They wait. They are known to be extremely patient creatures that also have a strategy. They will bite a big animal and since they have a lethal bacteria in their saliva, the animal is poisoned but does not succumb immediately. So what does the komodo dragon do? They follow the bitten prey and wait. Sometimes they will nip the animal several more times to speed up the process but even then it could take anywhere from a few days to a few weeks. But you know what? When the animal finally succumbs the komodo dragon is right there and begins the feast. Once they are done they leave what they can't eat for other animals and take a break. They don't have to hunt again for awhile because they are satiated and all else would be wasteful.

Rhayne, what the heck do those wildlife stories have to do with me? I am not following your logic. The logic in those stories are simple. As humans, we do not know when to let something go. Did you hear me? Let me repeat this. AS HUMANS, WE DO NOT KNOW WHEN TO LET SOMETHING GO. You don't believe me? How many times do you hear how awful someone's marriage is and how they are leaving but every time you see them they are still complaining about that marriage? How many diets have we tried for quick weight loss with the same results? Why don't we just go to the gym, eat with purpose and lose it gradually? How many things do we have in our home or closet that we need to throw away but can't because there is some sort of attachment, real or imaginary? And how many times have we replayed the same negative stories from fifty years ago in our heads, going over each detail trying to see where we went wrong? How is that productive? And you know what else? We tend to overdo everything, not knowing when to stop doing something and have trouble enjoying the present. Don't think so?

Why do we eat or drink until we feel miserable, then do it all over again knowing the end result? Why do we have eight of the same shirts in the same color? Why isn't anything we own enough and we always need more or bigger? Televisions, stereos, refrigerators, ovens, houses, etc are just a few examples. I am old enough to remember when televisions were black & white and had a 13 inch screen but it was great to be able to own one because they were considered a luxury. I know people who have

72 inch screens with surround sound, high definition, the ability to watch four shows at once and they tell me they can barely wait until the next best thing comes out when they haven't even enjoyed the now thing.

What is it about us that allows us to believe living in the past or doing the same things and expecting different results makes sense? Why do we hold on to those things that no longer serve us? Why do we want things, get them, use them once, then want the next best thing? Why do we think our happiness is based upon how many toys we own? Or that it is someone else's job to make us happy? Referring back to the animal examples above, can you now see what they have to do with you and I?

I grew up with very few luxuries and that was okay because I learned to be happy with small things and being my own best friend. Since I was my own best friend, I was never lonely or without company and I enjoyed being with me. Having less made me appreciate the times I had more and waste was never an option. Food is one of my favorite things in the world so I consider it sacred and never take it for granted. I will let it turn into a science project in my refrigerator before I throw it away because I feel guilty for not being able to eat it before it went bad. As per my last book, you know I am a yard sale junkie because I would rather reuse a thing of the past than buy a new item because it allows me to enjoy my need for nostalgia…and yard sales bring me a surreal kind of joy. Do you have any idea as to what makes you happy or are you just reliving the past when there were "better" days?

"If it's not breathing does that mean it's dead" is a metaphor for how we go about our days doing the same tasks, expecting new results and trying to resuscitate non working issues. As a matter of fact I think that may be the definition of insanity. We get up everyday trying to breathe new life into the same old issues by the same old methods. Animals seem to know exactly when something is no longer needed and they move on to complete another task. Animals evolve based on their environment and they change locations based on needs. If an area offers minimal food or shelter, they go to where those things can be provided; they don't stay for the sake of staying when they know there are other options. Sometimes they aren't sure if there are other options but they use their natural instincts to go find out. Humans somehow get sucked into doing the same things day after day, month after month then do a full time job of complaining because we haven't seen any growth. The only reason I believe my life is more interesting than the average person's is because I have always done different things on a daily basis and staying stagnant scares me more than change. Not being afraid of change has allowed me to meet people from all over the world, try delicacies from places I've never even heard of, experience different climates, cultures and terrains, see things I had only read about and, best of all, broadened my personal horizons.

My Canadian-Ukrainian gem, Steve, has a saying that just makes good sense. He says that doing the same things over and over and expecting different results is like wiping your behind on a wheel. BINGO! Sure it may sound funny but it is as basic as one can get to seeing the truth of one's actions. Your butt will never get clean if you are wiping it with a wheel as it keeps going around and around. Aha moment, huh? So how do you know if it is dead? Not your butt, your actions. Sometimes that is simple to figure out and sometimes it can be a bit more complicated. Let me give you some examples. If you…

* Are in a relationship of any kind and the other person always leaves you feeling drained, disrespected and/or worthless, no matter what, then that relationship is probably lifeless.
* Have a job that makes you sick the night before and angry all day while at work, it may be time for a change.

* If what you eat seems to be making you gain weight, then change your food choices.
* Don't like your level of knowledge or abilities, look into educational/trade classes.
* Don't like the gym, find other means of exercise as there are hundreds.
* Are being told something and don't know if it's true, do some research to find out.
* Aren't happy, start with small steps finding out what makes you feel good. It doesn't always have to be the big things that count. Start searching your soul.

Henry Ford once said, "If you think you can do a thing or can't do a thing, either way you are right." This is another set of truer words that have ever been spoken. And just so you know, getting to the point where you know what's working and what isn't may be easy...the part that seems hard is trying to figure out how to change it or what to replace it with once you do know. Now begins our Spiritual journey together.

TRAVELING AT THE SPEED OF UNCONSCIOUSNESS.

This header is compliments of Amy whose name appears on the cover and it is essential for getting grounded. Have you noticed how fast everything seems to go but yet it still is not fast enough? I am old enough to remember when telephones did not have voice mail or call waiting. You got a dial tone so calling back, maybe several times, was your only option. I bet some of you reading this won't even know what a dial tone is. I also remember when phones had short tangled cords, rotary dial and each call was .25 cents per minute in the day, .10 cents per minute after 7:00pm and .05 cents per minute on weekends. We didn't even consider speed because we were happy we could talk to someone miles away for a couple of minutes just so they knew we were thinking about them. We also wrote letters because it was far cheaper to write ten pages and mail it for a nickel. It was also exciting to see the mail carrier because they might have a letter for us.

Now I'm going to go even further back to the time when I remember the soda truck and milk truck delivering those things to our home. Yes, wise guys, they did that in New York! The trucks were bright red, the goods were in six pack wire crates and the sodas or milk were in glass bottles. The drivers didn't speed to get those deliveries to you because they knew you were not in a rush to get it on Tuesday, 8:00am or it's free. It was fresh, the drivers stopped to chat and every Christmas each person in the neighborhood gave them gifts to let them know how much their services were appreciated. Every holiday was filled with anticipation as each one was special in its own tradition, decorations and season. Families cooked from scratch (turning basic ingredients into cakes, pies, etc), people dressed with ultimate care and families who were far away usually visited by bus or train because flying was very expensive and not many people owned cars.

Now take a look at our days. We are racing from one red light on one corner to the next, running stop signs, forgetting simple pleasantries such as please and thank you and not caring how our own behavior affects others. If we don't take into account how what we do affects someone else then how can we ever feel inner peace? A few years ago I realized that no matter how my day was I came home edgy, jittery and had trouble falling asleep so I started observing what I was doing. Well, I noticed that ninety-nine percent of the time I had absolutely no memory of driving from point A to point B and before I knew it, I was "there". I started noticing that everything I ate was gobbled down so quickly I didn't remember what I ate until I burped later. I was constantly rushing, racing, zooming and getting angry when someone else would get on my highway and drive either in front of me or behind me. My dad's rule was always this; the person driving too slow in front of you was an idiot and the person racing past you was a stupid jerk who was "in a hurry to go nowhere." At some point I realized I was officially both. So how fast are we really going in this day and age and how does it factor into Spirituality or lack thereof?

Fast. Faster. Much faster. I, too, am extremely guilty of this. Check this out: Not too long ago I had two days off in a row and I was adamant about enjoying them. On the first day I got up around 8:00am, rushed to the shower, washed as fast as I could, got a little irritated when the 200 miles per hour electric toothbrush wasn't brushing fast enough and then raced into my clothes to get downstairs. Downstairs to do??? Nothing. I had absolutely no reason to rush anywhere but it seemed so normal. Off to a fast food place, I race to the drive-thru window so I can??? Then I do 60 miles per hour out of the parking lot, 50 miles per hour down my 35 mile per hour street so I can inhale two hotdogs and a bag of chips that I didn't even taste.

What is the matter with me? Well it isn't just me because I saw other cars racing to the light, to the drug store, to the next corner with most of them on the phone or eating. So how does that affect anyone else, Rhayne? Um, reality check. If, in our haste we hit another car or person or we end up in road rage, wouldn't that affect others? What if we run our car into a building? Wouldn't that affect our insurance, the company's business and perhaps we might even get hurt? It's one thing to race around your own home and fall down your own stairs but it is a totally different thing to cause pain to someone else due to our own carelessness. If you think about it, when we are constantly in a hurry we can't get quiet and enjoy the things around us that might bring us peace and joy. Maybe, and again just maybe, that job we may not like would be a little easier to stomach if we started our days with ease. Even if that isn't true we might be able to see more options for getting out and finding a place we really want to be because feeling peaceful allows for your mind to seek clarity. There is no way you can think clearly or positively when everything around you gets on your nerves starting at 6:00am and never seems to end.

Tell me, how many times have you wanted to call someone back in a day or two and by the time you get to it six months have gone by? How many times have you said, "I can't believe the year is almost over. It was just January!" How many times have you been meaning to go on your dream vacation and never made it? What about all the times you've been meaning to spend time with someone but time gets away from you and it never seems to happen? Let me shed some light on this as it is very near and dear to my heart. At age 43, I have been to more funerals than most people have been in three lifetimes. I have lost countless friends and of course it hurts me to say farewell but I have never had to regret not keeping in touch. I try hard to call and just leave a message at least once a month so they know I'm thinking about them. Now should be even easier since we have text messages, cell phones, email and cheaper travel. Do you have any idea how many loved ones attend the funerals and just bawl because they had "meant to" call that person and now it is too late? Yes life gets in the way but that should not be an excuse for unintentional negligence.

I can bet I am busier than 95 percent of everyone I know but I still make time to catch up because I am grateful that GOD has given me so many wonderful people that I just love. Everyone is always telling me how busy they are when their idea of busy is an eight hour work day with eight hour television nights. I travel three weeks per month, have a part-time job, a writing career, a singing career, rental properties, a husband and an 87 year old dad who lives one mile up the street from us, so that "I'm too busy" line doesn't work on me. The funny thing I noticed is how the folks who are always "so busy" seem to always find time to call when I can be of some assistance to them. Hmmm. Funnier thing is that they don't understand why I had to remove them from my life.

Remember the list of friends at the beginning of the book? Those friends play an active role in my life and they make my life even more exciting than it already is. Go back and re-review their characteristics so you can see the common and not so common threads amongst all of us. I even love their differences because I get to learn new things that add more knowledge to my arsenal of goodies. I have been asked on many occasions if I like one friend more than the other and the answer is always no. Each one is totally different, each one fulfills different things in me as a person and keeps me growing. All of us have learned to agree to disagree which was easy because they always agree with me since I am always the voice of reason! Hahaha! What a gas! And what a crock!

My mind is always racing with ideas and my body always needs to be in motion, so when friends began telling me on a daily basis that I needed to slow down, they just added to all the other annoyances. But, they were truly onto something. Slowing down is THE most impossible thing for me to do and most of the time it makes me nuts but I can see how it is effective in my daily life. If I have to meditate I want it to be during Boot Camp Kickboxing and not during Yoga where the sound of other people breathing makes me want to scream. When I pray I would also like to do it during eating and singing but it just gets garbled. Spirituality (and my husband & friends) has taught me how to s-l-o-w down without it being a chore and knowing how to enjoy it. I learned through many facets of religion that meditation is my chance to have a conversation with GOD and like all the other people I talk with, I do not engage in other things while talking because it doesn't lead to good results. I cannot hear if I'm doing several things at once and I believe GOD cannot tell me what needs to be done if I'm not paying attention. Besides, it is just plain rude.

Every exercise has its purpose and I attend each one with that in mind. In Yoga I should be benefiting from listening to my body and not someone else's. In Boot Camp, I am letting off all that nervous and toxic energy that makes me want to run everyone else off the road with my truck. In Zumba (high intensity multicultural dances) and Bellydance, I am getting in touch with my sensual side while enjoying being the strong woman GOD created. With all of these in place, and a few others, I am becoming the balanced person who can only go forward to do great things for others, and for myself. Once I realized I could be in balance, even with day to day mishaps, I knew I could also affect others in a positive way on a daily basis as well!

How does my balance and peace allow me to affect others in a positive way? I am less likely to get into an accident or confrontation if I keep my cool. My smile seems to tell others I value them and in return, they smile. I can offer kind words and/or compliments without feeling the need for return. I may be able to show someone that even though life may look a tad bit bleak, there is hope and help them work on a solution. I am less likely to feel insecure and others feel comfortable confiding in me. I am not that raging lunatic others avoided because they thought I was crazy. I am more apt to attract those who have the same loves in life and can help me go to the next level. Others enjoy being in my company and are more likely to help me achieve my goals. Can you see how getting grounded is a win-win? Good. Next chapter.

MAKE SPACE. EVERYWHERE.

A very important factor for receiving Spiritual enlightenment is the ability to create a clear and welcoming space for yourself. When I say space, I mean literally, figuratively, psychologically, mentally, socially and every other "ly" you can think of. If there is no more space how can you add anything new?

I am great at creating space for new things in my house, room and any place else that is physical. There are times when I just walk into a room and know there is too much stuff laying around that needs to be put away, put out or moved around. Sometimes it isn't things it's color. A certain color may make your space feel crowded or uninviting. I love color and I am not afraid of painting a wall in whatever color feels good no matter who says I shouldn't if I one day want to sell our home. How can you live in a place that doesn't appeal to you just because a future buyer may not like a wall color? How does this help you to relax and enjoy your surroundings? My husband is never surprised to come home and find all the furniture gone and paint cans on my ladder. In the end we both have a beautiful home worthy of enjoying when we come home for the night.

Sometimes you don't even know where to begin when there is too much stuff, and trust me, I know. For me, I usually start in my closets with clothes I haven't worn in forever. I go through my clothes with a good feeling and I remove items knowing that once I donate them, I am helping someone to have a new outfit that might allow them to get a great job or feel better about themselves. I clean my closets out with music playing in the background, me singing and before I know it, the task is over and I am ready to go through that stuff under my sink. Then I can vacuum. And dust. And clean out drawers. The entire time I am thanking GOD for giving me so much and allowing me to bless others. When I am done, I feel ten pounds lighter.

Now I am going to tell you what space is hard for me to clear out; and that would be the one in my head. My head is filled with things that constantly punish and abuse me and will not allow for the great things to shine. Those space takers rob me of my dignity, energy and self respect. Those cluttering thoughts keep me from going forward because they constantly remind me of mistakes I made in the past. How can I clean out my mental space when they keep adding other junk for me to take on? How am I supposed to get a clear head when the negative thoughts grab onto more negative thoughts and put them on the front burner while the good thoughts sit in the back row? Where do I start? Unlike moving physical clutter, this is impossible. No, it isn't, which is another reason I wrote this book.

I have been adding and subtracting things from my mind for years now so I can become a better me. Where did I start? Well, it wasn't easy because I had absolutely no idea where to start and it is ongoing but it is getting accomplished. I started reading books on Faith, meditation, eating for maximum performance, exercise, the human body, the mind, the soul, the spirit, color therapy, blood types and addictions. Because I didn't have a clue where to start, I read anything and everything that might add some insight. I also tried chanting, yoga, affirmative prayer, television evangelists, children's shows, jewelry making, false eyelashes, road trips and solitaire. Do you know what began to happen? I began to get bits and pieces from each source that challenged, inspired, intrigued and educated me. I learned about things that somehow seemed to nourish my soul and made me delve further into other things that seemed interesting. As I learned more I came in contact with people who I could openly tell about my problems and they gave me more information. Before long I had many things going on that I became good or better at and the thoughts that once told me I was useless started becoming less true and had to take a vacation.

Once I realized I was not alone in my fight for my mental sanity, I treaded into deeper waters mentally. I have always been a physical risk taker but in any risk, I never let my mind play a part unless my risk failed. If it failed, my mind would beat on me all the time and then bring up all the other failures so I could see that I had a running track record of being a failure. Obviously those thoughts made me acrimonious and kept me guarded. It wasn't until I met Pumpkin that I was taught to look at all of my successes which have far outweighed the failures. Who thinks of that? I did not even know that was an option. Why didn't I know? I didn't know because all of my young life I was always criticized for every mistake and rarely praised for any success. Of course I had no idea that was the reason until I started soul searching and asking questions. Every question lead to more questions and eventually I realized that the only way for me to move forward was to release the hurt and pain from the past.

Many, many books, people, internet sights, television shows and research said to "release the pain" but no one really explained how. I was told to pray, meditate, sleep more, eat less, ask GOD to take it out of my mind, tell the devil to let go and many other things were tried but didn't do the trick. I hated not getting control and hated having my husband stand by watching helplessly. Then I got sick of advice that obviously had no thought behind it. As a matter of fact, I was so sick of people prescribing things to me, including telling me my thoughts weren't real and how I was misinterpreting them, that I sent everyone an email telling them I was sick of it and to stop sending me ridiculous advice. You know what happened? No one responded. No one except my Canadian diamond, Joan. And Joan didn't respond right away as she was, unbeknownst to me, setting the stage to my healing.

Joan called about one week after my email and said in her always cheery voice, "Why aren't you coming to see me for my birthday?" Since I was truly a force to be reckoned with emotionally, I said, "I didn't even know it was your birthday. When is it?" Joan went on cheerily with details, telling me she was booking me a one way ticket and we would get a spa treatment, nice dinners and some girl time. Of course I agreed as she had me with the nice dinner.

So two weeks later I get to Canada and off we go to the spa, to restaurants, dinner parties and a million other activities Joan had planned. Then, six nights after I arrived, Joan and I sat in the same two comfy chairs that we sat in every night, in our cuddle bums (pajamas as per Joan!) and chatted like always. Joan asked me how I felt and told me she was concerned when she received my email. She noticed I didn't sleep while visiting and that wasn't good. We talked forever and after we were done, Joan hugged me. No, it wasn't just a hug. It was a hug that I had never experienced before. It was real and maternal. It was a hug that only someone who loved you and understood what you were going through could give you. It was also a hug that I wouldn't have let anyone else give me because it meant putting down my guards and that was one of the only things which kept me from falling apart. That night I slept soundly knowing that my husband had been right all along. I was a good person, I did matter and I was capable of being loved. It was that night when I finally understood what family really was and knew it was okay to trust because this was the only way I was going to get past the pain.

Joan not only got behind my wall that night, she allowed me to open my heart to others who had been loving me as much as I would allow. I saw openings where I could give more love in my marriage, to my other wonderful friends, to the new friends Joan and Steve brought into my life and, most importantly, to myself; the last person I trusted to love. My husband was the first person to change my life but there were just some places he couldn't reach, and that's when GOD sent Joan. Not only did HE send Joan, he sent her husband, their kids, their friends, their knowledge, their culture and exposure to Canada. HE cleared away all those people who were not helping my life and, because I had more room, HE brought in new ones. I was having trouble with my vision and HE brought Jim and Moni (my optical folks) through Joan and Steve and corrected my problem. Actually, this information segues nicely into the next chapter so let's not hesitate.

(FYI: Amy is another one who has that strong maternal touch and I wondered why she didn't respond to the email but when I looked back at the email, I didn't include her. Hmmm…)

I Manifest My Universe!!!

I know it seemed a little abrupt the way I wanted to get to this chapter from the last but it was necessary. As part of my Spiritual journey I learned from many sources the power I possessed to be able to manifest what I needed and/or wanted as long as it was good for all involved. Did you get that? What I may need or want has to be good for ALL involved. My interpretation of that statement? My gain should also benefit someone else. I realized I have always tried to make my decisions based on others getting a blessing as well, even if they don't know it. I also learned that the world I live in personally was manifested by me personally so I don't have anyone else to blame if it isn't what I want it to be. Author and Spiritual advisor, Catherine Ponder shed plenty of light on that for me. If you don't know her work, I highly recommend you seek out her books!

Catherine Ponder hammered into my head that in order to change my outer, I had to change my inner. I had to concentrate on what I DID want and NOT what I didn't want. I have always known this because I have always stepped out on Faith without worrying how things would work because I just knew they would. And they did. The trouble began when those negative voices started replaying themselves causing so many distractions until I got away from being able to just trust Faith.

Over the years, and my friends can attest to this, I have manifested employment, college scholarships, wellness, food sources, cheaper rent, different friends, travel and my husband. As an artist, I do things to my own beat so when I believe something, I really believe and I do not let go until it comes to fruition. Over the years many non-believers have laughed and waved me off but they are always the ones asking how I did what I did while they are still in the same situations. I tell them they have to believe and they tell me I'm talking nonsense. Funny thing is, all the people who tell me my Faith manifestation is a hoax are firm believers in The Bible. I always ask if they really believe in The Bible, how can they not trust Faith? Isn't Faith the staple of most religions? The answer is pretty much the same…one has nothing to do with the other. Really? I seem to remember many verses in The Bible that talk about Faith. Isn't it Romans 4:17 in The Bible that says, "…calleth those things that be not as though they were?" Or Matthew 17:20 that states, "He replied, because you have so little faith. I tell you the truth. If you have faith as small as a mustard seed, you can say to this mountain 'move from here to there' and it will move. Nothing will be impossible for you." Anyway, the truth for me is that I believe because I have seen it work in my life. The difficulty is trying to stay focused and positive when all of those past demons continually create the illusion of fear as rhema.

Manifest your husband? C'mon Rhayne. No, it is true. I told GOD years ago that I was fine with being alone but if HE wanted me to have someone I had a list of things I wanted too. I wanted him to be over six feet tall, dark and handsome, enjoyed my sense of humor, was quiet because there was no room for both of us to talk, kind, considerate, romantic, spontaneous, classy, a one woman man, non-drinker, non-smoker, non-drug abuser, non-abusive, didn't care that I hated domestic housework, loved unusual animals, enjoyed food & travel and took me seriously as a creative being. GOD gave me **ALL** I asked and more. HE added tolerance, patience, infinite love and sanity to Brian because HE knew he would need it. For over thirteen years Brian has listened to me talk nonstop, watched me juggle 500 things at once while declaring boredom, tended to a rabbit, fiddler crabs, hermit crabs and a lizard, lived with and without furniture, watched me perform, tried food he would have rather stepped on and all the while, smiling and nodding. Oh, did I mention GOD also gave Brian a sense of humor? Definitely necessary.

Other manifestations:

I needed $3000 to move from Virginia to Georgia and three weeks before the move I hit a lottery for $3500.

I needed to finish my degree at a cost of over $62,000 and I got a job where my boss would pay the tuition if I kept my grades B or better. I graduated in the top one percent of my class.

Joan and Steve, who brought Jim and Moni to solve my eye problems and Moni, who is a fantastic cook, appeals to my love of food. And they have full refrigerators. YUM-EEE!

Joan and Steve who give me so much knowledge about staying focused and getting to my dreams. And motorcycle enthusiasts just like my husband. Just so you know, I met them in a motorcycle shop in Las Vegas and three months later we flew to Canada to bike together. That was one week after praying for someone who could teach me about investing and adventure.

I was lonely in Las Vegas and asked for a friend who would need me just as much as I needed them and two weeks later Amy came along in a water class at the gym.

Years ago I had a surgery and somehow, the health insurance company lost my file and the hospital attorneys were coming after me to pay the $100,000 plus bill. I prayed for an answer and a few weeks later a woman I worked with on a part-time job told me she worked for that health insurance company, all out of the blue. I told her what I had been going through for over eight months and she said she would look into it. Within three days, she found my file as her department was a missing file department. She submitted the file so the hospital could be paid. The very next day, my boss from a company

I had worked for when I had the surgery years prior called to tell me that somehow they had mixed up the paperwork back then and he found my old health insurance information had been prematurely closed and if I had any old medical payments that needed to be rectified. Yes! I told him and he called the woman in missing files and the hospital's attorneys and everything was paid in full!

Now how is that for power! Okay, Rhayne, I get that, but…you're telling me you've always manifested good with your thoughts? Oh no, my good friends! I am telling you that my mind brought to me exactly what I concentrated on all the time. And, just so you know, it hasn't been just good either which is why I can tell you to do all you can to keep your thoughts in the now, in focus and in positive. So I guess you want to hear what I brought to me that wasn't exactly my idea of fun? Sure, why not.

When the voices in my head take over, I have a very hard time trying to stay positive, which is what the voices want anyway.

Examples of manifestations in reverse:

There were many times when I went to auditions with the mindset that I wasn't talented and wouldn't get the part. Not only did I not get the part, I sang miserably.

There were performances where the voices assured me that I would forget the lyrics and be off key. They were right and each song became more and more stressful.

I once bought a very expensive pair of eyeglasses and my family swore I would lose them because I didn't deserve them. That thought consumed my thinking until one week later I was walking down the street when a gust of wind swept them off my face, dragged them across the street and they were ruined.

It was a Friday evening after work and I needed cash since I was on my way out of town. As I stood in line at an ATM, the whole time I was thinking how much I hated ATM's and their stupid lines. When I got to the ATM, I put my card in and the machine kept it. It was 6pm so the bank was closed and I was standing there furious with no cash for the weekend.

Since I do not want to harp on the negative, this will be my last reverse story but it is a biggie. Growing up I had been constantly told that no matter how much I wanted to be rich, I would always be poor, would always lack money and would probably lose homes and cars to repossession and foreclosures. Over the years that message is one of the really powerful ones that has stayed with me haunting my every waking and sleeping moment. I have to be extremely careful about financial lack thoughts because I have noticed over the years I am at my worst the last three days of the month and the first five days of the month. Those days represent the times I am most likely to "screw up" my finances because I am "too stupid" to have money and the losses would serve me right for wanting to be financially independent.

For over twenty five years I have been battling those demons whose only purpose is to keep me from reaching my financial potential. Whenever I have allowed them to rule over all other thoughts, I almost end up in complete financial ruin. And, those demons are still factors today. Although they aren't as powerful as they once were due to my ability, most of the time, to see them as false, they still exist and they continue trying to keep me from achieving my goals. The positive is that I finally **know** what the problem is so I can continue to work on diminishing their power. I attribute this knowledge to everyone I have spoken candidly with, all the books I have read, getting the Spiritual ability to hear GOD through meditation and positive reinforcements. All which have come as a result of clearing my mind to make space for the good information.

So, Rhayne, all I have to do is stay positive and focus on what I want? I cannot say it is that cut and dry but that is truly a good start. When you wish to command something remember to make it good for others as well. If you want millions of dollars, think of how you can make a difference with it. If you want generous relationships, know that you, too, must be generous. Here's a good story. Carmen is and has been one of my longest and best friends ever. There have been times when she has gotten me out of some pretty tight spots and has never asked for anything in return. I, on the other hand, couldn't get Carmen out of tough spots because she's too smart to get in them in the first place so I return the love by calling her sixty times per day, mailing her cards, picking up trinkets and other niceties.

I worked at a company in Virginia where the majority of staff were women and the personalities were divided right down the middle; half were overly maternal and the other half only thinking of how a situation benefited them. I became the one person they couldn't understand because I didn't care what anyone thought or what anyone did as long as it didn't concern me.

Over time we became one big family, started to look out for one another, celebrated our good and bad days together and gained some trust. Carmen had a habit of feeding my love of unusual objects and mailing them to me at work from her job in New York. Every other week I would receive quirky shoes, unusual handbags, interesting pictures, non-practical jewelry and outrageous floral arrangements. All of my coworkers found this fun except one and she couldn't understand why anyone would do those things so she finally asked. "Rhayne. Why does Carmen send you all that stuff?" "Because she knows I love it." Then she adds, "I wish I had a friend like that. I would get everything I could from her." I was taken aback, irritated and insulted, so I responded, "And there in lies the reason you don't have any friends and can't keep a man (another killing a mosquito with a bazooka moment). You are so busy trying to use people and being selfish. Carmen and I have a give and take relationship, not a take and take. And as long as you are trying to get over on someone, you are *always* going to be miserable and have all those problems you are always complaining about. You have to **be** a friend to **get** a friend." And off I go. By the way, this incident occurred before I had peace, thank you very much. So what happened?

Since everyone felt the same way but I was the only one who had say it out loud, she became angry, embarrassed and suddenly aware I wasn't alone in those jabs. Two weeks went by without her speaking to me but after that she called me in her office, shut her door and said, "You were right. (aren't I always?) I hate the way I feel and I'm sick of being alone but don't know what to do. You come in here and act like life is always great and it gets on my f**k..g nerves. But at least you're living. I thought a lot about what you said and I am going to start working on being a better person. I'm sorry you hated me." I looked at her and said, "I never hated you. I actually like you. You have a good spirit. You're just miserable and that's too bad. There's a lot of good stuff under that misery." She hugged me and I went back to work.

Over the course of three months she became a new person. She lost weight, dressed better, smiled more and got a nice guy. I was really proud of her because she deserved better but she needed to see that her space was crowded by pain and anger that needed elimination. The moral to this fine story? You may not know where to start to get rid of clutter but the main thing is to just start somewhere. Start with your closet or your bathroom or one single thought that annoys you. Trust me, it is very easy to get overwhelmed if you try to tackle everything at once. Make a list of just <u>one</u> thing you want to clear away <u>today</u> and <u>today</u> <u>only</u> and be proud of yourself when you do it.

Things that worked for me:

* Playing my favorite music while sorting out only ONE thing at a time (closet, drawer, etc)

* **Keeping my purpose of space cleaning to myself (limits naysayers)**

* *Giving with a smile*

* Getting rid of "fat" clothes (increased my self-esteem)

* Took classes that challenged my abilities (pole dancing, yarn spinning)

* Looking at what I was tossing out & thinking if a friend may need it

* Asking my husband to clear out his space; in his own time (it was contagious!)

* Painting & redecorating a room

* Yard sales!!!

* Positive conversations with like minded people

* **Self praise**

* **Being kind to myself when I make a mistake**

* Books of all sorts to open my mind

* Exercise in any form & doing it with a smile knowing it clears my body

* Travel (car trips, walks, info on the internet of where I'd like to go)

* Learning a new language

* Learning a new word once a week

* Watching children's cartoon

* **Take notes on what I get in return when I give freely & without attachments**

* **Being grateful**

Being grateful is such a big part of life that I am going to give it its own chapter. I hope you are enjoying my journey thus far and somehow it's all beginning to make sense to and for you.

OH THANK YOU!!!

Being grateful was one of the things deeply instilled in me from an infant. I was always told I should be grateful because kids in other places didn't have food or clothing. I should be grateful because some people didn't have arms or legs or eyes. I should be grateful that I had a roof over my head and a warm bed. And I was grateful. No, I am still grateful.

I have always been grateful because I think it is part of who I am as a person. Even though I was an only child at home, I always shared toys, clothes, food and money. I hated knowing that someone was hungry or without a coat. At age eight, one of my older cousins taught me how to sew and make all of my own clothes. It was a great form of self expression and when I wore an outfit, if one of my classmates liked it, I would give it to her and make another one. I was always grateful when someone thought of me as well.

Our landlady, Ms. York, grew the most beautiful roses in all colors on a trellis that wrapped around the entire Victorian porch and they would be blooming at their peak in June. She saw the way I admired them since we moved there when I was two years old. My birthday is in June and every birthday, until I left for college at age eighteen, Ms. York would clip only the most vibrant roses, wrap them in newspaper with a ribbon, ring our bell bright and early before I went off for the day. I would look down the steps and there she was with the biggest bouquet of flowers just for me! This was the first birthday gift I would receive every year until I graduated high school. Those flowers made me so thankful that I could see and smell.

Grateful. About twenty years or so ago, I can remember people always giving thanks for something. There were lots of thank you's, please, how nice and it's beautiful! Over the last few years I have noticed that the faster we go the less we seem to appreciate life and all that it has to offer. Thank you and please seem to be disappearing pleasantries from our day to day interactions. I watch people not hold doors for others, snatch money from others in transactions, bump into someone and not say excuse me and countless other ugly acts. I have also noticed that the more we get, the more we think we are entitled to have.

A lady I know and her husband bought their seventeen year old daughter a new VW bug for her graduation and her daughter was angry because she wanted a BMW. The parents were hurt so they took the VW back and got her a bicycle. Their daughter was distraught but the parents explained to her how they worked very hard to save for that car and since she was ungrateful, she would now have to work and buy her own car because they did not raise her to be disrespectful. A new car? I was so excited to have my ten year old used clunker that I thought I was driving a BMW!

Being glad for everything was never something I had to achieve because it felt natural but I want you to see how wonderful it is to be full of thanks. For as long as I can remember up until now, I have given thanks for every bite of food, for our home, income, clothing and our health. Some days things are going by so fast and there are so many things I want to see and do that I do get irritated when I don't get the things I really want and life sucks and there's no Easter Bunny and whaa whaa whaa. Those days get to me because something small will happen and I feel like a dope for undermining all I do have. The one thing I have a firm belief about is that being grateful DEFINITELY, WITHOUT ANY DOUBT, brings more and more of the things you DO want into your life. Besides, who wants to give you more when you aren't caring about what you already have? Or you don't enjoy your current gifts?

Remember the Carmen sending me the gifts story? Each time I received something from her I was just as excited as though each time were the first. Do you think she would indulge me if I called her and said, "I don't like red roses. I wanted white." Let me tell you, that would be the last gift and telephone call with Carmen. Over the years I have received so many wonderful things from friends and strangers until I cannot even begin to remember all of them but I can tell you this; no matter where I go in the world I have a place to stay and a meal and so do my friends as thanks is the gift that continues to give.

There are two other parts to being grateful; you must learn to give unconditionally and receive openly. Unconditional giving requires you to give without strings being attached, as said before. Many years ago there was a church friend who complained for years how GOD wasn't answering her prayers after all the money she's given HIM in church. She said she thought GOD would be more grateful than that. Hahaha! What a self righteous thing to say! That statement told me she gave money to the church just so she could have her wants answered. What about all the people and projects her money helped over the years? I'm sure that never crossed her mind because she was so angry with GOD's selfishness.

I had another friend some years ago that would "give" money then tell the entire world what she did for the recipient and how they were indebted to her in so many words. She, too, was always miserable and without understanding as to why she was friendless. Whatever you give you should give freely. Also know that because you give freely, you will receive abundantly in return.

Receiving openly can be difficult. How many times has someone given you a compliment with you turning it down? I don't do that Rhayne. Really? That's a pretty dress! "This old thing? I've had it forever…" You look great! "Ugh! I gained weight and…" Here's a little something I got for you! "No you shouldn't have. I can't take this…" Sound familiar? When someone gives you an honest compliment, gift or other, it is your duty to accept it openly and be thankful. I've learned over the years that when you accept a gift that someone decided was specifically for you, you should beam with light as it makes the giver feel as though they made the right choice. I have given gifts where the receiver told me they couldn't accept it because they "didn't have anything for me." Knowing me, I couldn't believe they thought I picked up the item expecting them to have something in return for me. Now that's something that doesn't cross my mind. I love seeing a specific item and picking it up for a particular person to enjoy. And you should have great enthusiasm when you receive a gift, no matter what it may be.

At one of my housewarming parties years ago someone gave me a set of kitchen towels with huge roosters printed on them. Roosters? For a New York City girl's home? Everyone there just stared at them wondering what on earth that guest had been thinking. I gave her the biggest smile, got up and immediately put them on display in my kitchen. Later that evening when everyone left except three friends who helped me clean up, one of them said to me, "Rhayne. You can take those awful towels down now, she's gone." I looked at her and asked why she thought I should take them down. "Those aren't you. They don't even match your décor." My reply? "I'm not taking those down because that woman didn't really know me but she thought enough of me to come and bring a gift. What a wonderful thing to do!" To me, the surprise is what makes the gift magical! And speaking of magical…

Let's talk about how holidays have lost what used to be known as celebrational bliss due to spending time with people you loved and/or the flavor of the holiday itself. Can you remember the excitement that came with birthdays as a child? The possibility of turning another year older and people you liked (or didn't like!) brought you gifts or sang to you was almost more than one could stand. I LOVED when my birthday fell on a school day because teachers brought in ice cream and cake so I could share with all my schoolmates.

As a matter of fact, this continued straight through high school and each one was just as spectacular as the one before it. Anita was the birthday celebration queen in high school. Every year, without fail, she would bake a cake that was or had chocolate on it and bring it to school. Days before she would delegate to other classmates what to bring on celebration day so at lunchtime on my birthday there would be lots of food, soda and cake for everyone. Just thinking of how much love Anita put into planning all those birthdays makes me teary eyed. Boy do I love that cute but tough little Puerto Rican girl. I also felt the same about my friends' birthdays. I would get so excited when I would think of the look on their face when I presented them with their favorite cupcake or slice of pizza. And you know what else? We never snubbed each other no matter how small the gesture, we were just happy to be in each other's company.

I am a very proud graduate of Music & Art High School, class of 1984, in New York City as that school changed my life forever. You see, we were a creative arts school and any chance we could get to stretch our creative legs, we went all out. Birthdays were monumental as were every holiday and every upcoming anything. We had gotten so good at enjoying each other that we celebrated Mondays by getting french fries at a local dive and Fridays by ordering one big sandwich and splitting it among five or more. We even arrived at school 45 minutes before class so that several of us could go to a popular sandwich dive to get a Mammy Jammy to split. A Mammy Jammy was made in this dark storefront with one greasy light bulb by a gentleman from the South who used the softest hoagie bread lined with ham, cheese, tomatoes, pickles, lettuce and mayo. So what was so great about that Rhayne? What was so great??? That man pressed the sandwich in a dry cleaners pants press so the sandwich would be hot and toasted! MMMM-MMMM! We didn't care about germs because we were celebrating life! I think we had those sandwiches at least three times a week and we never tired of how much laughter it created. Or that we had cast iron stomachs that fought off salmonella. Those sandwiches bring back the best memories but it didn't stop there.

Holidays. Sweet, sweet holidays. As a child I thought every holiday was a chance to celebrate seasonal changes, temperatures, costumes and food. Kindergarten made holidays heavenly. So many songs and crayons and sparkly things and costumes! Halloween was always my favorite with Christmas and the fourth of July bringing up the rear as I went through great pains to make sure everything was in order for each day. Halloween meant spending days figuring out my costume character! Pumpkins were so bright and shiny! (not my husband, the actual vegetable).

Trick or treating was the best as I always received money because I didn't eat candy. The fourth of July meant parades in Manhattan and rainbows of fireworks. Christmas, for me, started the day after Thanksgiving and my mother was worn down every year with me wanting to put the tree up that day. All the lights in the city, crisp winds, ice skating in Rockefeller Center, carolers, food smells in the air and Santa Claus! Santa Claus kept me from sleeping for days knowing he would come to my house and leave me fun things under my silver aluminum tree that flickered with bulbs of all colors! The excitement was overwhelming!

As I got older I still had the same enthusiasm and zest for life and at Music & Art, I found many other creative souls who enjoyed life just as much as I did. Music & Art was made up of teachers and students from all walks of life who came together as one big family. Our teachers, though strict about making sure we learned, were just as exciting when it came to enjoying life and allowing us to be who we were. I was exposed to some pretty amazing facts, information and ideas through creative learning and tough but necessary love.

Our teachers taught with a fervor that had to be there to keep creative students from taking a mental vacation during classes which spilled over into holiday celebrations. Choral classes sang original birthday songs, performances were geared towards holiday events and we decorated our school (the Castle on the Hill) with whatever we thought reflected the holiday. We came in costumes on Halloween, put up Christmas decorations to represent all nationalities, celebrated Hanukah with menorahs, Easter with egg hunts and we even had Flag Day ceremonies. I can't even remember what Flag Day was about, all I know is that I was having a good time. And, we were thankful to be a part of such a great school. Then we graduated.

Once I became an "adult", people urged me to "get serious and stop that celebrating foolishness" because there were "more important" things to concentrate on. The first couple of years I continued celebrating but noticed it lost some momentum as I was one of the few who kept office parties alive. By the time I turned twenty-one I noticed that holidays were becoming less important and birthdays even less than holidays.

At age twenty five I moved to Richmond, Virginia where the communities still celebrated arts, holidays and whatever else they could come up with. Talk about being rejuvenated! I was a duck mascot for a radio station, a polar bear for the grand illumination of lights the day after Thanksgiving, a student in jewelry making, a learner of fondant, a participant in the Watermelon

Fest and anything else I could find in their local paper. What? Oh, I'm sorry. The Watermelon Fest is a weekend festival in which they close down several blocks in a trendy shopping neighborhood and worship the Watermelon. There are live bands, international foods, shopping, laughter and, of course, Watermelon prepared in hundreds of ways. Mmmm-Mmmm! A haberdashery of culinary excellence, I say, ol' chap!

My point to all of this? The joy of being thankful for today, all the gifts it gives you and you receiving them with real grace. If you go back and reread the above stories you will see that gifts aren't always tangible and they aren't always obvious, even though they should be. Teachers who cared whether or not I would go on to do great things were gifts. Laughter is a gift as well as friendships and experiences.

One of my favorite and most cherished gifts are memories. Even the not so good ones as they taught me what I didn't want to experience again. It isn't the holiday itself that should matter. It isn't the surface stuff or the price of a purchase that matters. It isn't how good or bad a meal was that matters. What matters is the gift of the memory the day created for each person involved. I believe that over the past few years we have seen life whizzing by because, instead of enjoying the now memories, we are looking for the next set of memories and we never stop. I am known to send a birthday card to friends at any time of the year because I know their birthday has to be sometime that year but it is just a card to let them know I am thinking about them. I'd like to think that when their birthday is in March and they get my card in November it always makes them laugh. It also makes for funny conversation when we finally see each other after years of misplaced cards.

I have outlived many of my friends and I can't remember many of the gifts I have given them but I can remember the sound of their voices and the look on their faces when I told a joke. I am so thankful to have the gift of my senses. There are times when a smell takes me back to being a little girl playing in dew covered grass in Appomattox, Virginia in my favorite great Aunt Julia's yard. Or a song by Candi Staton that puts me in Philadelphia in 1976 at my cousin's house who loved to entertain. And the gift of touch. When I was five, I was visiting my grandmother's farm and I touched a cute, fluffy chick that decided to peck my hand full of holes until it looked like a water sprinkler. And what about the gift of being able to remember? I did part of my college internship in a nursing home and my heart used to ache for the elderly that tried to remember people and places. They would have given anything to recall a name or a place.

Before I close out this chapter I would like to believe that after reading this you will try to take a little time everyday to see how fortunate you are and give a little prayer of thanks. I would also like to suggest that even if you can't seem to find something to give thanks for, then give thanks for being literate so you could read my book and pass the blessings along to others.

LISTEN TO THE SILENCE.

Doesn't that sound like an oxymoron? How can you listen to something you cannot hear? I am with you on this one but it is a crucial part of being able to go inside yourself and find yourself. Distractions keep us from being able to focus on ourselves and acknowledging our true feelings. When we are distracted we are easily thrown off our course. How many times have you gotten up with a list of things to do only to be derailed by an unexpected glitch? Can you recall how the initial glitch opened a path to other glitches that just threw your entire day off thus creating agitation? Wouldn't it be nice if you could sidestep those unexpected events and keep your focus on what you had to do in the first place? Or at least keep your cool knowing that you cannot control everything?

Silence. It is such a holistic word that, upon saying it, can bring you mental peace in any situation. It, for me, was a learned word and a learned practice. I cannot stand the thought of extreme quiet, especially when I am alone because that's the time my mind runs amok. Before I started meditating my mind kept me in a constant frenzy. Thoughts were so out of control that by the time night came I was exhausted and just dropped in the bed. I am sure all of you can relate. Your mind will tell you nine hundred things that need to get done now; bills that aren't paid, money that needs to exist, clothes that need washing, a wallet that needs finding, a squeak that needs oiling, hair that needs washing and a bathroom that needs cleaning, all at the same time or you aren't being productive. I used to spend more time grasping at my thoughts than I did at accomplishing anything and my mind made me feel guilty for listening. Then someone tried to introduce me to meditation.

Yes I said tried because the first few years of trying to meditate were seemingly a waste of time, especially for someone like me whose insouciance towards life couldn't understand why the process was necessary. I took classes at churches, schools, houses, street fairs and I always got the same results. As soon as I became a little quiet my mind would bring up all the things I had to do immediately and it was off to the races. Here is a little fodder for you. When a noisy head like mine used to go to a meditation place and someone wanted to interrupt it with silence, the anger was unbelievable. How dare they bother my noise with their quiet? And how dare they try to stop me from having a stroke, a heart attack and high blood pressure? It was just plain inconsiderate.

After a couple of years of useless quiet I met someone who told me I didn't have to go somewhere to get quiet. Huh? I could embrace the things I already loved, totally lose myself in them and then the silence would follow. I was asked, "Have you ever gotten so entwined in something that you forgot if anyone else was in the room?" Interesting. With a new piece of wisdom I started to become more aware when I was alone in a crowd. Yard sales, botanical gardens, museums, operas, projects where I'm building something and the ocean.

I could clearly see how removed I was from noise when I was engaged in those activities so at least once per week I made sure I became a part of those things I enjoyed. As a matter of fact, it was what I did every Sunday. It even became a ritual that created vicissitudes without me forcing them into existence. Slept until 10:00am, a breakfast of my favorite in season fruit, comfy clothes and off to the place that was calling me. Lunch consisted of tea with a scone and by 4:00pm I was so relaxed I could face the rest of the week with a smile. Of course, based on where I was living there were variations but I kept to Sundays and I kept to a regimen. We know life can throw curvy roads but this is a necessary regimen. I also find that because I have catholicity, it is easier to find many things that please me on a daily basis.

There have been many times where I just haven't been able to find a place that feeds my silence and let me tell you, the days just get more and more intense and I can feel how different I respond to the same issues. When I have taken in silence I can usually respond with affection and clarity. Without, I am a raving lunatic who can part the Red Sea with a glare. With, I can over boil a pot and just start over. Without, the pot and everything on the stove goes in the trash or out the window. With, I can eat sensible portions and feel satiated. Without, I eat a serving for nine and then get mad because I knew better. Rhayne, this sounds like someone who needs a prescription. You are absolutely right! It is a prescription but a natural one from the Universe, available to everyone at all times, if we can just figure out how to access it for ourselves. And like you, I am still learning the process. But each day brings a little more progress so I can go to a class and participate as though no one else exists. I stop by trees and smell their flowers. I get in my vehicle and smile when the air conditioner comes on when it is 109F degrees outside allowing me a cool ride with cool thoughts.

The three biggest bonuses for me now that I can listen to the silence are these: I know I cannot control everything. I can only do such much in one day and the rest will get done the next day. And I DO NOT feel any guilt! Secondly, I can hear all the great ideas GOD has been trying to tell me so I can be a better me. All of a sudden I have lots of ideas on how to earn extra money, pay off that one big bill or create a book. I am sure HE was trying to get those to me before but I was too busy being busy. Third and last, I get a good night's sleep. It is amazing how a sound night of sleeping can make you feel like royalty the next morning. When I was "busy" I didn't know I wasn't getting good sleep because I was always tired and I thought that was just what happened when you worked hard. Wrong! That is what happens when you don't have any peace.

I have to tell you that while you are trying to listen to silence your mind will conjure up all sorts of garbage to keep you from settling down. You will experience old hurts, anger, defeat, defensiveness, delirium, depression, confusion, shame, weakness, anguish, lack and denial. Please trust me when I tell you that ALL of us have done something which makes us feel bad so don't let those false emotions appear real in your journey. If you stick with listening to the silence you WILL emerge stronger, smarter, happier, confident, abundant, focused and full of joy for each day. I am also going to tell you it was NOT an easy or short journey BUT, it has been worth every false emotion I had to overthrow to arrive! Just take it one emotion at a time, one silence at a time and you will surprise yourself with the results.

***I hope you noticed how cleverly I threw some words in this chapter that we probably don't use every day but they make for fun reading, mental stimulation and a good excuse to dust off your dictionary!

Cow Udders & Chickens Or...
Not The How...It's The What.

Might I continue to pontificate (another word for your mental massage!), let us speak about cow udders and chickens or not the how it's the what. I can only imagine what is going through your mind as you try to figure out what all of this has in common but I assure you they are all relevant for your next step.

I read a very intense course outline book titled, The Master Key by Charles F. Haanel, written many, many years ago which walked me through a slow course in mental awareness so that one may bring what they want into their life. After a few weeks I arrived at a chapter which read, "You are simply to say what you desire, not how you are to obtain it." That statement stood out for me because I could remember times when I had no idea how something was going to happen, I just knew I wanted the requested results and they appeared. But, over the years with too many negative voices, I seemed to have lost the ability to concentrate on the what and gave too much power to the how. The very next day Steve sent me an email that read, "Rhayne, just focus on the what and not the how. And get very clear about what you want." Whoa! Was that not the ultimate confirmation? How did he even know that was what I was doing or how I read that somewhere the night before? Clearly this was GOD and His Universe using them to give me direction. So where does the cow and chicken come in? I bet the suspense is killing you so I won't make you wait any longer.

Cows have udders that give milk. Chickens lay eggs. Neither of them have ever asked how they do it, they just know it is *what* they do. Wouldn't it be nice to have that same knowledge and not try to figure it all out? Could you imagine how things would go if the farmer came out at 4:30am to gather eggs and get milk and this was the scenario: Cow: "I want to give a nutritious drink from my udders that helps humans but I don't know how. Hmmm. I wonder if I ask around maybe one of the other farm animals could tell me?" Chicken: "I sure would love to lay a thing that could become another chick or maybe even be a source of food for humans. I wouldn't even know where to start and besides, that sounds like a nutty idea. Maybe I'll ask around." Pig to the duck: "Hahaha! Did you hear that chicken? And what about that cow? Hahaha! Those two come up with the strangest stuff. How the heck are they trying to lay a thing to eat or create a drink?" Duck: "I don't know. Even if their ideas were logical, how would they begin?" And so on and so forth.

The bottom line is that there would never be any eggs or milk if the animals had to figure *how* they were going to do it. And even if they did figure out how, the peanut gallery would probably keep them from accomplishing their goals because they are non-believers in the what. Rhayne, you are being silly. Farm animals would never have such a conversation because giving those things is what they do. Okay. Good point. But…isn't fulfilling our dreams what we are here to do? Do we not have things we think of that we know we want to do more than anything on earth but once we start trying to figure out how we lose heart? Or, once we run it by others who think it's a terrible idea we give up? Do you see the correlation?

Concentrating on the *what* and not the *how* makes total sense when you get right down to the core of it all. How is such an overwhelming word when trying to make good decisions, or any decisions. How is one of those words you have to use sparingly and with a clear head. Here are some good how examples:

* How am I going to pay for school?

* How will I ever get this house clean?

* How many hours will I have to study to pass that exam?

* How am I going to lose twenty pounds?

* How am I going to become a _____?

* How am I going to pay all these bills?

* How can I afford my dream vacation?

* How am I going to tell my family what I want to do?

Any of those sound familiar? By any chance, do they give you a feeling of panic and dread? Have they kept you from doing the things you wanted to do? <u>How</u> is a word you have to break into tiny little pieces in order to digest. My husband and I have a funny thing we say that we heard somewhere years ago when one of us gets overwhelmed by a how situation. We say to the other, "How do you eat an elephant?" Answer? "One bite at a time." Taa-daa! Now doesn't that sound simple? Any and every situation is much easier if we take it one bite at a time. Some situations may not need you to bite at all when it first appears, it may only need clarity about the **what** which can seem simple but really can be tricky.

When I think about what I want I usually end up thinking about all the things I *don't* want and then I get all flustered. Example: "I want to be on television but I don't want to be in a drama show." With that statement I am sending mixed signals and things don't move in the direction I want because I am asking for two conflicting actions at once. A better way to say it would be, "I want to be on television. I want to be in sitcoms and cartoons." Now that is better because it is clear and to the point. I have not left anything out but I also did not get bogged down in the how. "How can I be on television? How do I get in a show? How am I ever going to compete with other actors? How, how, how!" and then I sink back into not doing anything because it all becomes too much. What if I started by reading a book or article on acting? Or see if a local theater will talk with me. Or ask around to see if anyone (in that field) knows anyone who could steer me in the right direction. Maybe if I just put it out there in all sincerity, ideas and situations will appear as long as I don't panic and try to control every single step.

Like most of us, I want to have some control over *how* I am going to go from where I am now to where I *want* to be. Lots of times I get annoyed because I am trying to force something that isn't supposed to be forced. Perhaps repose is what is needed to free your **what** to the Universe and make it start taking shape. Remember those how situation examples above? No matter what, if the house was dirty you found a way to get it clean. When the bills were due they got paid. One day you were trying to figure out how to go to school and get through all those tests and the next day you were graduating. You see, one small step will get you where you want to go. The hard part is usually thinking about **how** you are going to take that step. But if you do, you will take another one and before you know it you are on your way. And also know that there are going to be ups, downs and obstacles so keep your eye on your want. I read somewhere that 98 percent of people quit right before the payoff because things looked too bleak or got too hard or they were encouraged by loved ones to give up. Isn't that what would have happened to the cow and the chicken had they taken farm advice? Instead, they continued to do what they were doing, without complaining with benefits for all. And speaking of complaining...

LIFE'S NOT FAIR WHICH IS WHY BRAS & JOCKSTRAPS COME IN DIFFERENT SIZES.

When I was in high school my friends and I came up with that saying and we used it anytime one of us was whining about whatever. Thirty years have passed and it still applies today as we all have unfair episodes and excuses should not keep us from success.

Bras and jockstraps. Isn't it funny how those items were the most important things to us as teenagers? We were really stressed about how we were underdeveloped, overdeveloped, too short, too tall, acne, eyeglasses, personal style and being accepted. I can remember tailoring my outfits so they covered up what I didn't like and accentuated what I did. Where did I get that kind of time? Why did that even matter? I don't know why I just know that it did.

I also remember my teachers not taking excuses about life not being fair. "Life isn't going to be fair. Life is going to be exactly what you make it. If you fail to plan, then you will plan to fail." Truthful words spoken to us everyday by one of our teachers, Ms. DelValle. She was strict, tough and one heck of a teacher. "If life doesn't go where you want it you will have no one to blame but yourself because you didn't plan." More great words by Ms. Ellis, another teacher who was tough but great. Looking back, those statements were preparing us for the real world because they cared about us and knew we wouldn't get to our destination if we didn't have a destination. Or in the words of another great teacher, Mr. Lurtzman, "If you don't know where you're going, why should you care where you end up?" I'm not sure if those quotes were theirs originally, I only know that was where I heard them everyday for four years of high school.

Excuses are easy ways to cloud our vision; I can't because. I don't know how. It's too hard. I know someone who tried that and it didn't work. It's a stupid idea. I don't have time. I don't have money. I'm too busy. It's not a big deal. I don't care about having a lot of money. People who are rich are never happy. Money doesn't buy happiness. I like being big and curvy. I don't care about travel. Do any of those ring true with you? If they don't I am sure others do. No matter, they are all excuses designed to keep you from getting what you want. Some of those are even packaged as jealousy.

I am proud to say out loud that I want to be wealthy. I have been saying this since I was a little girl. I also noticed that many times when I said it people felt the need to tell me how rich people weren't happy or they don't care for having lots of money or, the most popular, money doesn't buy happiness. Now here is my problem with those statements. The majority of people who would say that were always complaining about how they never had enough to pay their bills. They were the same people who had their hand out when they knew someone who did have money. They were also people who didn't really know anyone wealthy to have a fair assessment. I knew they really wanted wealth but they were not sure how to get it or they didn't want to do the things required to achieve it. I have often heard those same folks talk negatively about those who were living their dreams.

My husband and I work very hard, try not to make excuses and we get very disturbed when someone feels they have the right to tell us that "money doesn't buy happiness" but they are always looking for a handout from us. My retort is always, "You're right. Money doesn't buy happiness. But neither does poverty." What money can buy you is freedom. The freedom to go where you want, when you want and how long you want. It gives you power as well. The power to help others and yourself. And because money is so powerful, it can make life more fair for you. Money can help you accept your bra and jock strap size or allow you to alter them to your liking.

Money should not be used to buy happiness and should be used as a vehicle for the good of all. Remember I mentioned that earlier? Remember I also mentioned there were many wealthy people in The Bible? While we are on the widely uncomfortable subject of money, let's expand what I think money really is and what it really means.

Over the years I made the discovery of money being such a great energy that, like religion, it could turn people towards or away from one another. It could produce or cease anger. It could give or take away. It could create or destroy. It could come and go without notice. It could make you powerful or leave you without any control. What it wasn't was a replacement for what makes you truly happy or who you truly are and I believe that is where people get confused. Somewhere money went from being a source of buy and sell to own and dictate.

My personal experience with money is that it can make you emotional which can make you do things you might not have thought about prior to having some or none. I've watched money (having and/or not having) turn people into misers, control freaks, out of control spenders on non needed items, snobs, liars, cheaters and thieves. I have witnessed money turn people into philanthropists, charity organizers, world travelers, missionaries and world changers. By the time I was in college, after observing countless money transactions, I came to the conclusion that having money intensifies the person you really are anyway. If you were a kind giver then it seemed to make you more giving. If you were a little condescending then you became a real jerk. These have just been my own personal observations so don't get too bent out of shape as it is just food for thought. I only want you to think about how you feel about money for yourself or when you see others with it.

Money doesn't have a life, we give it life which is why I want you to examine how you feel about it and how you treat it. I, personally, feel that money is good and richly enhances the ideas and desires *I* have in order to feel complete. Read that again carefully. **For me**, money *enhances* my ideas and desires, it DOES NOT create them; the creation comes from inside. And just so you know, not everyone needs a lot of money. *I*, based on the dreams and goals *I* have, will need a substantial amount.

I do my best to respect money as I always try to keep an open flow by genuinely giving and genuinely receiving. My experiences in life show that when I am not giving, I am usually not receiving and I don't always mean money. When I forget to give I notice there is a congestion in my ideas and many other places where I usually see growth and inspiration. My life lessons have taught me that I cannot receive unless I expect to receive. Again I am not talking about giving in greed.

I certainly know people who only give if they think there is something in it for them. Give freely from your heart, know that because you give freely you will receive freely and make sure to be thankful in all you do receive. Just think of it like many of life's other gives and receives or balances, such as; a bathtub holds a certain amount of water when there is a plug in it and in order to add more water, the plug must be removed to start the release of what's already in the tub so more water may be added. Need another one? How about the human body? We eat and drink but we cannot do it without our bodies releasing what we have already put in to make room for more. When we give our bodies too much and no release happens then we experience a stoppage of the natural order. I sure hope this is making sense to you because it is necessary knowledge for your growth on your journey.

Money is not the thing that makes life fair or unfair but it does have the ability to tilt the scales a little for you so you can make it more comfortable for yourself. Know what else has the same ability? Kindness and respect. And those do not have a price. If everyone extended kindness and respect to their fellow persons, the world would be so much calmer, plus we probably wouldn't be so concerned about what is and is not fair. What does that mean anyway? Who sets the standard for fair? Could that be just another fraudulent editorial acting real?

I want you to pick up a fashion magazine, flip through it and then think about what you feel. If you are like me, I never feel tall enough, rich enough, thin enough, fashionable enough or beautiful enough. Life isn't fair because I'm not 6'1" (I am in my mind!). Life's not fair because I have hair on my lip. Ohh boo-hoo! Life isn't fair because those women have it all. How would we know that? Aren't those illusions of what life should be? What do you think about yourself without those images? Being taller or thinner never seems to cross my mind until I watch a music video or see a magazine spread. GOD made me just the way He wanted me. I am supposed to focus on what I am good at and not what I am told I'm supposed to be good at. I am 5'3", strong, funny, intelligent, healthy, a great entertainer, a real person who cares about others and a force to be reckoned with when I notice injustice. I am never going to be tall and thin so going through life with a chip on my shoulder about it is insane. What I can be is great in my own right as long as I keep my eye on who I am and not on who I should be by the world's standards.

Last year I read an article about James Dyson, the gentleman who invented the dual cyclone bagless vacuum cleaner we all know as Dyson Vacuum. I want you to look up his biography as it is a real story of passion and persistence. Mr. Dyson had been working on his invention for over twenty years with many let downs but it did not stop him. As you can see today, his determination was rock solid and paid off. When I finished reading his story I thought to myself, "All those years for a vacuum cleaner? Why didn't he invent something else as he was obviously a very smart man?" Then it dawned on me. The invention of his vacuum cleaner was *who he was* as he saw it to benefit many others. He probably could have invented anything else he wanted but his heart, soul and drive were immersed in this one vacuum that could change the world of household chores and he wasn't about to get sidetracked. His story changed the way I felt about my writing ideas and my singing career. If Mr. Dyson could be that dedicated to a vacuum (his destined creation) surely I could be more determined about my future as a multi-faceted entertainer. I believe he had no idea how his invention was going to come to be but he was certain that it would come to be because that was exactly *what* he wanted. Get clear about what you want and life will be very fair to you.

So let us talk a bit more about getting clear. Isn't saying to myself, "I want to be an actor" clear? Think back to the cow and chicken story chapter, when I quoted The Master Key and Steve. What I learned was in order to get clear and precise, you have to make a list or maybe even fifty lists which state all the things you want. Once you make a list you cannot be vague about your desires because your wants appear as a result of how badly you want them from the INSIDE. I can almost guarantee that if you only want something in passing you will not get it as it has no real importance to you so concentrate with your entire being on what you want.

You may also need to keep your ideas and wants to yourself to minimize any outside interference leading you astray. Your list may have only one or two items or it may have twenty items. Look at them and ask yourself if those are the things you really desire and if they are specific. Can you close your eyes and see them in your mind? Let's take the actor scenario. You want to be an actor? Break it down to its lowest common denominator (high school math!). What kind of actor? Comedic? Dramatic? Live theatre? Movie? Film? Television?

If television, what types of shows? Commercials? Sitcoms? Soap operas? Do you want to be full or part time? Are there certain roles you really would like to play? So now you have a really good idea of what type of actor. What next? What is required to get the roles I want? Acting classes? Move to a big city? Need an agent? Need audition material? Get my drift?

Please remember this is not a project to do all in one sitting since you don't need to get overwhelmed. Pace yourself. Look at your list all the time. Carry it with you. Study it. Put it where you can always see it. There will always be changes in the things you want so do not be afraid to add or subtract from your list. Steve swears by this and I, too, know that it works but only if you get really clear in your goals. Rhayne, based on what you are saying, you have achieved everything you ever wanted, right? No, but I am very close. Like I mentioned before, I let other things take me off my course so now I am getting back into the swing and I can see the goals on my list coming to fruition.

Lastly, cross off your accomplishments as they come to fruition which will make room for more and allow you to easily recognize what you have accomplished. Enjoy your achievements and be grateful for each tiny step you take knowing that it is leading you in the right direction. Stay faithful, positive and focused. Do not forget to guard your eyes, ears and especially your mouth as they hold the power to your successful journey.

Proverbs 4:23-27
(The Holy Bible — The Gideons International)

Keep your heart with all diligence, for out of it spring the issues of life. Put away from you a deceitful mouth, and put perverse lips far from you. Let your eyes look straight ahead, and your eyelids look right before you. Ponder the path of your feet, and let all your ways be established. Do not turn to the right or the left; remove your foot from evil.

Buddha Quote:
The tongue like a sharp knife…kills without drawing blood.

Jewish Quote:
Teach your tongue to say, "I do not know," lest you be led to lie.

Coup De Maitre!
(Better Known As Stroke Of Genius!)

Aren't you guys proud of me using all these big fancy words? Aren't you even more proud knowing that I know what they mean? Aren't words simply glorious? Aren't you glad you can express yourself with letters joined together in a pattern to let others know how you feel? And to top that we can learn other letters and characters which will allow us to communicate in different languages with people all over the world! Brilliant I tell you. But you know what is sad, girls and boys? It is sad that with all we are capable of doing, we do not do. We also allow personal prejudices, whether our own or others, to keep us from interacting with like minds. I am not sure if it's because of fear or ignorance. Let's go back to the wonderful world of insects and animals.

Have you ever watched insects or animals in a garden? Squirrels, butterflies, worms, birds, chipmunks, bees, flies, ladybugs, ants and all other creatures coexist among the trees, dirt and flowers. Each one is busy with a chore. Some are gathering pollen, some are digging through the earth while others are just enjoying all the pretty colors. They tend to stay out of each other's way, avoid being eaten by those who might need a snack and yet they still get everything done.

If you have seen this display then you should have noticed the beauty each one brings to the garden without others commenting. You've never seen the ants stop to gossip about the butterfly's breathtaking wings. You haven't seen a ladybug complaining about wanting stripes instead of dots to the grasshoppers. I can also believe you have never seen all the insects stop to tell an unusual participant to get out because they were different. I believe they all coexist peacefully because each one respects the other and knows that all of them are the reason the garden is so magnificent. Squirrels and chipmunks never wage a war based on who has more nuts in their possession. Bees don't act like bumper cars because they saw the flower first. And birds don't shun other birds because they aren't the right color. I bet you are thinking I am sounding silly again. Reread this paragraph and think of the human parallel and say it isn't true.

Animals and insects work in harmony because, instinctively, they know that each one's job is important to nature and there is no time for petty foolishness. They have "like minds" which is what makes them genius. If you are surrounded by like minds, you understand that you do not have time to dilly dally around because there is a bigger picture. As humans, we tend to get lost in who gets what, how much more they are getting and how we can up our gain instead of seeing the big picture. We somehow get involved with negative like minds and those can ruin your dreams.

Joan and Steve are firm believers in surrounding yourself with positive like minds. I have been doing that since I was a kid and because I am my dad's daughter, I sometimes lacked tact but I figured if someone was not good for me it was better to tell them to get lost before the games even began. Why drag something useless around if it has nowhere to go? It would be like getting a big wart cut off your nose then carrying it around in your pocket. It was not attractive to you on your face so you don't need to have it in your pocket as it serves no purpose except to constantly remind you how ugly it was on your face, and relationships are pretty much the same way to me.

So how do I know if I am in the company of positive like minds? Oh that's easy. Positive like minded people are always enthusiastic about helping you see your goals through. They are cheerleaders, editors, fans and great sources of information that they give readily. They are goal oriented people who are in the position you wish to be in or on their way and heading in the same direction. I am not talking about people who talk the talk but don't walk the walk. Observe the people you are interacting with. Watch their actions to see if they are really pursuing their goals or if they are just full of pigeon stuff. Observe their friends as well. Here is a good example of knowing the difference. Many years ago I was invited to a financial gathering that was supposed to show people how to become wealthy and secure. Since I am always interested in growth, I made sure to attend.

My thirty second rule came into play as soon as I drove into the lot. When I arrived I took notice of all the cars parked in the lot with the company's name on them. Hondas, Neons, Toyotas and one older Mercedes. Then I noticed the people in charge were wearing wrinkled shirts, shoes that weren't shined and untidy hair. Once the seminar started the "financial gurus" started telling everyone things like, "we, too, could be extremely wealthy like them" and "we could drive dream cars and travel on private jets" and a bunch of other stuff I wasn't buying. Well, as fate would have it, in this room of about 300 people the head guy saw me sitting amongst everyone else, pointed to me and said, "I can see by your face that you are a non believer young lady. You do realize that in order to have wealth you must have a positive attitude."

Like my dad, I am not one who misses an opportunity to embarrass someone in public so, with bazooka cocked to mosquito, I stood up and calmly replied, "Sir, you may be fooling the rest of these people but you cannot fool me. First of all, if you and your colleagues are as rich as you claim, why is everyone wearing all of those cheap suits and runover shoes? And how are you driving a ten year old beater with nearly bald tires? And last of all, why is this meeting in this grubby hall with flyers that have misspelled words on them? There is absolutely no way anyone in here can teach me how to become wealthy because from where I stand, you're in worse shape than the average person. Goodnight and good luck."

As I was leaving several other people left as well and told me how they thought the meeting was a joke but didn't want to say anything. One lady said to me, "I didn't want to be rude so I would have stayed the entire three hours." I looked at her and told her I could be doing something else that was real and not sitting there wasting my time with a bunch of con artists who are insulting people's intelligence. She then said, "I wish I had your guts." My retort? "Ma'am, if you don't stand for something don't you know you will fall for anything? Stop letting people waste your time because you will never get it back." My dad used to tell me that all the time as he was most certain people were "full of crap and will put it in your mouth for as long as you will hold it open." Could it be any plainer?

Another great thing about positive like minds is that they genuinely care what happens to you. Even if they don't understand what you are trying to do they support it anyway because they see the joy it brings you. My friends are extremely instrumental in my ongoing success as they tell everyone they know about me, my books, my singing and magically, doors began to open that weren't there before.

I can count on all the folks I described in this book not to mention countless others that cross my path on a daily basis. I do not put any energy into those who are negative, needy, controlling, bias, prejudice against race, sex, religion, etc. nor do I try to "make" a relationship that doesn't exist. I see so many folks making excuses for a bad friendship or marriage because they want that relationship to work so badly. Is it really okay to trade your self-respect and dignity for a relationship? Is it even a relationship when you are the only one in it or it only exists in your mind? Healthy relationships naturally fall into place with each one giving life to the other (remember the balance speech?). A real friendship doesn't leave you feeling like the back end of the horse's cousin and it has no room for excuses as to why the other person behaves the way they do. I know it is only human to want to be loved but it can't be forced. Another example, compliments of yours truly.

I have a friend who is one of the most delightful and considerate people I have ever met...but...she somehow feels the need to make everyone she meets a "nice person." Well you know me and my thirty second rule. I have met most of the people she considers nice and each one has nothing to offer her. Most of the people can see her kindness from miles away, which they feed off, and/or try to take it away from her. She believes that all people are genuinely good and as a result people always end up hurting her. The worst part is that she somehow finds the exact reason for their bad behavior. If they come back into her life, she, again, gets the dirty end of the stick. I tell her all the time that she has to start guarding her heart.

I know she is looking for love but that truly is not the way to find it. Over the last couple of years I have watched her watch others and she has started seeing people for who they truly are so that she can pull away immediately. My friend leaves me in constant awe at her ability to openly love anyone and that scares me because she has so much to offer the world but she wants to give to those who don't want her love, leaving her in constant question. I really think she is getting it now. Everyone is not interested in being a part of your positive light so don't waste time shining it on them, go find people who are lovingly like minded so you can make their lives better and yours as well. She's working on it!

I want to interject this as well. Notice I add positive before like mind. I did that because negative like minds congregate as well. Another quick story. Another friend of mine, about ten years ago, constantly complained as to how she couldn't get her life together, she tried to stay positive and wished she could be more like me. Look here gang, don't say you want to be "more like me" because I can tell you that what you see is a result of many trials and tribulations. Get clear and make sure you know exactly what you are asking.

Anyway, she asked for my help. We started getting together and I instantly noticed something. Her family had a negative comment disguised as a compliment for everything, no matter what anyone was talking about, including her husband. Comments like, "You don't need that cake even though it is good." "That's a nice dress you're wearing even though it's better for winter." "The baby looks healthy even though he looks overweight." And it never stopped. No, I'm wrong. It did stop. It stopped so that each person could take a turn complaining about life, their job, their spouses, the house, the weather and everything on this planet. Okay, I am out of here.

The next day she called me and I laid it on the line about how negative everyone was and if she was going to change her life, she would have to change her company, even if only temporarily. She started making excuses for everyone that was in attendance and couldn't see how I came to the conclusions of their comments being negative. Yes, I know, hard to fathom but she asked. I broke it into small pieces, emphasizing the point that their comments were the reason she always felt bad about herself. Her response? "You just need to get to know them. They really do mean well." Since I know when a scraggly mop no longer cleans a floor, I removed myself from her company (yes I told her why) and when I saw her five years later, she was still complaining about the same stuff. Go figure.

Back to the positives. I am going to let you in on a secret. It is SO great that if I weren't a giver I would keep it to myself! Here is the absolute BEST thing about positive like minded individuals. Positive like minded individuals can and will teach or show you things you never even knew existed! There! That's the secret! My like minded friends have taken me to places I have only seen in magazines! They have introduced me to foods and drinks I didn't even know about! (and I know about food!) Imagine being introduced to things you never knew you would like because you didn't know you were supposed to! Let me take you on a friend stroll.

My Canadian diamond, Joan. Until I met Joan I had absolutely no idea I was supposed to be all dolled up to go, well, everywhere. When I started visiting Joan I was amazed by all the fun colors of girly stuff she owned. Lipsticks, eye shadows, fairy dust for your hair, glittery stuff for your toes, fluffy stuff for your pillows and feathery stuff for your outerwear. I was, and still am, amazed. Even though all that girly stuff amazed me, it was nothing compared to dinnertime and snack time setup.

I am, and have always been, a paper plate girl. It is no secret that I abhor washing a dish. I would rather throw it away and buy another plate than wash it. Not Joan. The very first time I sat at her dinner table I didn't even know where to begin. There were so many unbelievably beautiful plates, chargers, flatware, glasses and do dads I had to mentally go back to my fifth grade etiquette guide so I wouldn't drink out of the wrong glass. It gets better though.

All during the day and night Joan puts out snacks in some of the most gorgeous dishware known to man. There is a different sparkly dish for pickles, potato chips, candy, nuts, fruit, flowers and eggs. How the heck did one women figure out how to dress up potato chips? Each snack also had its own picker upper. There was a pickle fork, a candy spoon, an egg cup, hand carved salad utensils, shrimp pokers and some other poking things I had never seen before. By the third day I told Joan she didn't have to use all that stuff for me. She said, "Oh. I do this everyday." "What?!? Why?" Joan looked at me matter-of-factly and replied, "Because honey, I like it. It's pretty. Don't you think so?" I couldn't believe my ears. All those lovely things being used on a daily basis just because she likes them?

If you read my book, Gracie-isms, you know I was brought up to only use the "good" stuff when company came. Joan had decided that she and her family were the company. How AMAZING was that??? I had to think back to all the people I have known who ended up never using their "good" stuff because they were waiting for the "right" time. Joan had decided all the time was the right time. Well I'll be a donkey's mule! After many visits with Joan I saw other things I didn't know I needed. Translucent egg timers, teabag holders, coffee spoons with dangling gems, lip plumping glosses, cheek color palettes, brushes to groom my face to perfection, a cosmetic bag with a handle and, a pet buffalo. Somehow I must have needed a few of those unidentifiable objects because I keep seeing new stuff in my cart when I run to a department store.

Since I've known Joan for a few years now, I am almost positive that before I met her I didn't have an olive skewer, a teabag drainer, a cucumber shaver, anti fungus nail polish, a table setting for four, custom salad forks or fuzzy throws for my sofas. Until I met Joan I didn't even know I liked those things. But you know what? Not only do I like them, I use them everyday because they are pretty and I am the company!

My friend Alix offers a different type of like mindedness. Alix is a total free spirit who, like me, gives everything that one time try just to admit to doing it. Alix is so alive that when I'm with her I am ready to shed the inhibitions life has put on me without my permission. I am completely alive and ready for whatever. I never need much coaxing to try something new and I think Alix comes up with stuff just so there can be two of us on this planet who went the extra mile to be different. Since Alix lives in Arizona I give her plenty of notice as to when I will arrive because I know that will give her time to find out what's going on, where, when, how, who and then she makes choices.

The last few times I saw Alix we ended up thrift store shopping for hours, trying a new, chic raw bar restaurant, standing in line for three hours at night at a carnival haunted house to celebrate my favorite holiday, Halloween. We ended the night with funnel cake and pizza for dinner. Alix knows the best eateries, 5am yard sales, rocks to climb, fishing holes, dog parades and meditation studios. I took my magnifying glass with me last time and every spot in Arizona had Alix's footprint on it.

Alix is artistic in every sense of the word. Her style is cutting edge but not abrasive, her personality is strong but light and her spirit is all encompassing. Rhayne, you sound like you're describing yourself. Aw shucks. Flattery will get you everywhere but let's stick to Alix because the affect Alix's like mindedness has had on me has been wonderful as well. I remember how life isn't so serious and no matter what, just enjoy the journey, including the rough patches. Her enthusiasm never ceases to amaze me and her spontaneity keeps me on my toes.

Okay, this is my last positive friend story. My friend Olga is also my belly dance and Zumba instructor. Olga is from Russia so culturally we are miles apart. Of course that didn't stop me from wearing her down. I started classes with her a couple of years ago and I made sure there was never a dull moment in her classes. A funny thing when I started taking her classes; I was petrified of dancing. I could not imagine my clumsy feet doing international dances or my entire body grinding to some Mediterranean chimes. After a few weeks I became aware that I wasn't too clumsy after all and started taking more classes. Before I knew it I was doing Zumba and belly dance six times per week! I was getting good and now I am even better. Olga never lost patience with any of us which made her classes easy, fun and natural feeling. The biggest bonuses were my new feelings of confidence and sex appeal. All those moves leave me feeling sensual, feminine and accomplished. Olga's classes always offer positive energy, humor and exposure to music from all over the world that stirs my soul. I ask her to say things in Russian because who knows when I might take my belly dancing skills there for a winter party!

Try to keep in the front of your mind that some people come into your life for only a specific amount of time and once they have given you what you need, they will go. Don't try to hold on, just let nature take its course. So that's it. I'm done. With this chapter I mean. I hope my stories gave you a clearer understanding that **you are what you surround yourself with** so do your best to make good choices. Who knows? Maybe it is time you went on a people diet to help you shed that excess negativity!

An Experiment.

When I was in college one of my colloquial classes gave us an unusual assignment with the intention of "changing the way we view life on a day to day basis." Even though that assignment was over twenty years ago, I remembered it because it did change many of my daily perceptions and now I want to pass it along to you.

My professor gave this experiment assignment:

> * Let us say you had to live the next twenty four (24) hours without one of these; sight, sound, touch, taste, speech or smell. I want you to first tell me what you would remove and why. Once we finished telling him then he said that for the next four (4) hours (length of our class) we were going to honor our decisions.??? Yes, whatever we told him we could live without he covered so we couldn't use it and we would go out with chaperones to see if the world felt any different to us. I chose not being able to hear because I just could not imagine not tasting, not talking, no sense of smell, unable to feel or loss of sight so that had to be the lesser of the group. Please remember this class took place in New York City and when the experiment was over, these were my results.

With my ears completely sealed off from sounds, I hit the street feeling totally lost. New York City is a place where there are constant sounds from cars, trains, people, animals and things you just cannot describe. Because the loss of hearing was so abrupt, I had trouble keeping my balance. I felt like the world was leaving me out and pushing me aside. Although I still had my sight I had trouble crossing the street because I was used to listening to hear what was coming. At one point I didn't even see a gigantic fire truck until after

I got on the other side of the street. While walking with a few of my classmates I was well aware that I was missing things others seemed to catch. Jokes, laughter, information, guidance and the hotdog stands. No those are not audible but somehow not being able to hear the hotdog as it touched the bun bothered me. Asking for help was so frustrating because people are in a rush and me not being able to hear just got on their nerves. I decided four hours had to be close but when I saw a clock I had only been without my hearing for thirty minutes. Did loss of sound slow the world?

By the time three hours was up we were corralled back to class, unmasked and had to give detailed descriptions of our experiences and what we learned. I listened to classmates who chose loss of sight and I couldn't believe they thought that would be easy in the beginning. Some of their experiences were so traumatic they cried while telling their stories. When it was my turn I gave the above experience along with feeling like I had vertigo the entire time which kept my stomach in a constant state of nausea. What I learned surprised me.

Since I've always given thanks for having all my senses, limbs and other parts it never dawned on me the emotional toll a missing part could have on an individual. I am not saying that a person who is deaf feels this way but I felt like life found me invisible because I couldn't hear. If I asked a question in a store and couldn't hear the answer, people became annoyed as opposed to empathetic. If someone told a joke and I didn't laugh because I couldn't hear it, the person snubbed me as though I were a child, or an imbecile. How could something that could happen to anyone leave others so insensitive? Didn't they know they, too, could go deaf?

I even remember some teenagers making fun of me when I was doing sign language. Their exacts words were, "Look at that girl! She must be retarded!" How were they taught to ridicule something so serious and so frightening? I realized most people were either too busy to cope with another person's handicap and/or shortcoming but, even more profoundly, I saw that my inability to hear made them feel vulnerable. I suppose if they saw a young girl like me without the ability to hear they knew it could happen to them as well and they would no longer be immuned. Out of sight, out of mind...just in case it was contagious.

Now I want you to try this exercise even if only for one hour to get an idea of how your life would be if you woke up one day without that one ability. For me, without my hearing, I would miss birds, leaves, water, my husband's voice, my friend's chatter, talking on the phone, movies, footsteps, rain, the doorbell, car horns, music, food cooking, laughter and thousands of other things I may have taken for granted. So that night when class was over and ever after, I made sure I put extra time in hearing EVERYTHING.

I never missed anything before but the things I once considered a bother pre-assignment were now just as important to me as the ones I considered pleasant. When I pre-screen an excuse I make sure my mind goes back to that experiment so I can recall how I could be trying to accomplish the same goal but without my ears or eyes or legs and it would still need to be done no matter how difficult.

With those things in mind, why would I spend another minute not getting busy doing the things I want to do right now? I learned first hand that if I continued to wait to pursue my dreams I could lose precious time, my health and/or my abilities. My biggest lesson was to be more considerate to others because I never know what they are going through and I might be the one person who makes their day shine.

PART ONE: LET ME BE ME.
PART TWO: I WILL GIVE YOU ELEMENTS
OF SURPRISE!

Let me be me. This is a lesson I learned from my husband. If you let people be who they are I can guarantee things will be much better for everyone. I hope you are understanding those four little words because they are a very strong dose to swallow all at once. Let me be me.

But Rhayne, I do let me be me. If that is the case then why do you only do the things that make others happy? Or why do you ask everybody in sight what you should do in a decision that only affects you? Like a new haircut? Or a new dress? Women ask me on a regular basis what I think the key has been to Brian and I being together for almost fourteen years. My answer? "He always lets me be me." Most women say that their husbands do the same but when I ask if they can go out and do something they enjoy on a whim they tell me they have to "run it by him" to see what he thinks. And what if he doesn't approve? Then they don't do it even if it is in their best interest.

Another common case are the women who tell me they let their husbands be themselves BUT, unlike me, they would "never let their husband ride a motorcycle." How are you going to decide not to let another adult do something that brings them joy? How did you get that right? You want to know how I think you think you got the right? Even if you don't want to know I am going to tell you.

One of my biggest pet peeves are people who complain about their spouse's habits, manners, hobbies, etc and how they want to change *them* but there is never any mention of changing *themselves*. Story time.

One of my friends constantly complains about how her husband "always leaves the toilet seat up & he never holds the door for me & he spends his weekends watching sports…" I ask my usual question in that scenario. "Did he do those things when you were dating?" "Yes." "So what's the problem?" "Well, I thought he would change once we were married." Or…the other most common complaint I hear. "Before we got married my husband used to do x, y or z and now he doesn't. Once you get married those things stop." And men ask me questions too. "Rhayne. When I met my wife she worked out all the time and now she has let herself go. Why?" Or, "Rhayne, I loved riding my motorcycle all my life and as soon as we got married my wife wanted me to stop or get rid of it. Says it's too dangerous." I want you to know that the information I am about to give to you is relationship saving, changing and joy giving but it is also only my personal opinion so do with it as you wish.

I always thought I would be the last person anyone would come to for relationship advice but if I can change and become more accepting, then so can you. First of all, I have watched the dating process and I know people like to bring their representative to the dates. Who is my representative? What is this woman talking about now? You know exactly what I am talking about folks. Your representative. The person you dressed up physically and mentally so that you could make a good impression. You put on your best manners, your nice attire, your hair was perfect and so was your conversation. If you did not like what the date said you either ignored it or thought they were cute. If a habit was a little distracting or potentially irritating, you convinced yourself it wasn't a big deal or you would work on changing it at a later date. So you keep on dating. Then it gets serious and you move in. Ladies dream of a perfect wedding and men dream of whatever men dream about.

While dating, did anyone think to talk about things they enjoyed doing as an individual? Or did you discuss it, didn't like their choices but kept it to yourself because, again, you would fix it later?

So later came, you got married and your representative started to fade away. Or your perception of who the other person was may have been distorted because you wanted that relationship more than you wanted to see the real picture. Why do I say that? I talk to hundreds of people per week and many of them, especially women, go into a relationship starry eyed and in an imaginary love fog of how things are going to be. The only problem is that most of those things are only going on in your head.

Ladies, including me, believe that men are mind readers. I was convinced if I needed help with something Pumpkin would know and not watch television instead. Or if I told him how much I loved apples and he passed several farmer's markets while driving then he was just being mean and insensitive. How would he know what I am saying isn't what I am saying? After being irritated and telling him why I was irritated he would say, "Babe. Why didn't you just ask? You know I would have been happy to stop so you could buy apples." Hello, husband! How would I think of that with my woman wife brain??? That was earlier in the relationship and I have learned that instead of thinking Brian moonlights as a psychic, I just ask nicely. Like normal people. But before I was married let me tell you how I dated.

I would go on a date, wear the styles I would normally wear and acted the way I normally acted. If a guy had an annoying habit, I would make note of it. I also had a "deal breaker" list in my head of things that would make the date over instantly and permanently. My top two were, if he wanted to live in New York forever and/or, if he wanted kids. Date over.

But Rhayne, how would you have known that? Easy. I always viewed dating as a way to get to know what I wanted, did not want, would or would not tolerate or what I would and would not accept.

Dating allowed me to evaluate the other person to see if he was compatible for my lifestyle and needs. You didn't answer the question Rhayne. How did you know if he wanted kids? Easy. I just asked. Plain and simple. Dating was like a job interview. You start with light chit chat, ask pertinent questions then decide if that person is a good fit for you. If not, why waste each other's time when the date has nowhere to go?

Can you believe how many people would criticize me for breaking a date off because the guy wanted children? I always heard, "He was a nice guy and would have made a great husband. Why didn't you just see where it was going? You might have changed your mind." Do you know what? FOR ME, some things are NOT negotiable, with having kids being the first. I never said the guys were not nice because most of them were and they probably would have made great husbands. For someone else who was looking for a family man. Not for me and that was that. My other misunderstood deal breakers were men who wanted a housewife, control freaks, chauvinists, womanizers, smokers, drug users, alcohol abusers and under six feet tall.

**WORTHWHILE NOTATION: While I was growing up, the women in my family (and their friends) always said, "Half a man is better than no man at all." And, "All men cheat or drink or fight. You will have to put up with something." As a child I thought those were some of the most ridiculous things I had ever heard. My dad used to tell me "I could do bad all by myself and didn't need a man to help that along." I think the only reason I could not wrap my mind around the half a man thing was because I saw, firsthand, the way those relationships panned out.

I watched men come home whenever they pleased, horrific verbal abuse, terrible womanizing and all the while the wife was okay because half a man was better than no man at all and every wife had to put up with something. These were women who chose their clothes, hairstyles, makeup, fruits and veggies with extreme care so they could get just what they wanted and there weren't any exceptions. A rotten apple was a rotten apple and no fruit purveyor could convince them to buy that apple, or even take it home for free. A rotten apple would never have been good enough for a homemade pie. So why was a man, or a half a man, good enough for their homes and children? Why did they feel they needed a man so badly that they would "put up" with anything? I decided way back then that they had exactly the man they accepted and if they liked it, I loved it. I just knew those man choices were not for me and someone had to change the description of relationships. And that someone would be me. Now back to our regularly scheduled story.

After years of visual and internal assessments, I figured out that the women who stayed on my case about dumping nice guys for unimportant reasons were the same women who ended up in relationships where the men treated them poorly. Their dating process was different than mine. Ninety eight percent of my friends and their friends that dated went in with, what I thought, poor criteria. They weren't on the date to screen for compatibility, they were on the date looking for a husband. Reread that, I'll wait. Do you understand the difference? I dated to make sure I got what *I* wanted **for me** and not looking for a man to accompany me in my perfect mental wedding.

While dating to "look for a husband" they intentionally overlooked disrespectful behavior, bad manners and future hang ups because it would take them away from their goal of a fairy tale. I have watched terrible dates turn into awful marriages and my friends want to complain to me knowing my response. "You wanted a husband so you got a husband." (Isn't that just another version of accepting a half a man?) Rhayne, that is a terrible thing to say. No it isn't. It is honest. You will get what you accept and the other person will give you what you will accept.

I have been on dates where the guy started making subtle comments about changing my style and/or personality. DEAL BREAKER!!! If he is brazen enough to start that crap *before* he really gets to know me imagine what would happen if I married him? Never again would I be able to be me all because my representative didn't take his ill comments seriously. Rhayne, you might be too critical. Maybe so. But you know what? I got exactly what I wanted in a spouse and in my marriage. I wanted respect, someone who liked me just as I was, supported my dreams, worked hard, was over six feet tall, was a one woman man, never left the toilet seat up and laughed at my humor. And because I respect myself, he goes the extra mile to treat me like a queen by opening my door, helping me with my coat, giving me flowers and countless other displays of affection. All of this *and* with my dignity, self respect and self worth still intact. You know what I had to learn in return? To let him be him.

Brian LOVES motorcycle riding. I'm sorry, I meant, he LOVES riding sportbikes (in the world of bikes the terminology makes a huge difference!). I never understood why a person would rather be on a vehicle that exposed them to the elements and allowed bugs to hit their face with such force one could see what the bug had for lunch. Anyway, he loves it. In the beginning it made me very nervous when he rode but I kept that to myself because the look on his face when he suited up was indescribable. The happiness in his eyes was so intense I didn't need to know *why* he wanted to ride, I only needed to know *that* he wanted to ride. The look on his face was the same one I got when I saw a sign that read, "YARD SALE". He never said anything to me about digging in other people's junk because it made me happy and I wanted him to ride because that's who he is.

The women who tell me they wouldn't let their husbands ride are doing one of two things. 1) Killing his spirit, or 2) Making him resent you in the long run. The men who come to me and tell me what they will and will not let their wives do are creating the same issues. People need to do the things they enjoy, be who they truly are and then they can come together to enjoy everything else as a couple.

Trying to change your partner and/or control them only creates a venue for resentment, anger, depression, rebellion and separation. By the way, my degree is in Human Services and Social Sciences, my background was Social Work with eight years of diverse field training, so I had to study human behavior for a very long time. With that being said, I want you to know how unfair and selfish it is for you to decide to change or control someone because you went in with your mind closed and your eyes open. We get it Rhayne. So how do we fix it? You want to know how do we fix it, eh? (My Canadian accent keeps slipping in). I think I may be able to help you with that but the truth is, you may not like it. Or you may love it! Let's go people!!!

PART TWO: I WILL GIVE YOU ELEMENTS OF SURPRISE!

If I may continue to pontificate, perhaps we can get you on the right track to make this part of your Spiritual journey smoother. Just so you know, it is so much easier to figure out who you are and where you are heading when you have home support.

So, you are in a relationship that you aren't happy with and you believe it would work only if your partner changed. Let's start with that. Please don't forget, this is *your* Spiritual journey and *you* are doing things only you can control right now. Here are some questions to ponder:

* Do you think you should be trying to change your partner?

* Are you perfectly certain that the real issues are only because of your partner?

* What could you gain if you started to change?

* What is the worst thing that could happen if you changed?

* What is the best thing that could happen if you changed?

* Do you believe you can change?

Those questions have no right or wrong answers. I included them so you will take time to really think about what they mean to you. What's that? You want to know how I answered those questions? I guess it couldn't hurt to tell you.

I, too, thought I should have been working on changing my spouse but I did not realize that was what I was doing. To make matters worse, no matter what he did differently, I was still miserable so maybe the changes needed were my own. Then my minister's voice spoke clearly to me. "Remember Rhayne, Bless him. Change me." That was it. It was those simple words that penetrated every fiber of my being and changed my heart. Bless him. Change me.

I want to thank my minister because those few simple words saved my marriage and my soul. Those words became so powerful in my day to day actions. I said them at least three or four hundred times a day. Sometimes I said them with a smile, sometimes with a flood of tears, through bouts of depression and uncontrollable anger. Each time I said them I felt a calm come over me that would still all the pain. As weeks went by the voices in my head started making sense so that I was able to sort out what was truth and what was not. Talk about breakthrough! Finally I was able to figure out who I was and get the voices out of my head that were making me believe I didn't need to change. I came to the conclusion that those voices didn't want me to change because they would no longer be able to control me with fear.

Those four simple but powerful words brought a clarity so vivid I couldn't help but understand that my husband did not need changing but I did. Those words opened my eyes, allowing me to see that I was strong, worthy, determined and able to change. But let me tell you something serious. It was HARD. EXTREMELY DIFFICULT. There were so many surges of fear, disbelief, pain, anguish and loneliness until I was convinced I was going to die from a broken spirit. Gut wrenching emotions were the absolute worse things that happened during that time of internal remorse and turmoil. Here is more serious news. One day I woke up and there was less pain and more hope. I remembered an old Spiritual I used to sing in church that versed, "This, too, shall pass." Wow.

The day that song was playing in my head I was certain my "things" were changing for the best. Bless him.

Change me. Suddenly, after months of hurting, I saw everything in a new light! All the issues I assumed my husband had were gone because they really were my issues (fraudulent editorials acting real) and I began my journey of trusting with an open heart. I was exposed to new people who furthered my ability to love because now I was "lovingly likeminded." Other people who were fine with my previous pain started to fade away as we no longer had misery in common. I lost weight, worked out my finances without fear and started enjoying life all over again. Those were just some of the best things that happened once I transformed!

Did I think I could change? I had no idea. I knew something was wrong with me but I couldn't put my finger on it to change it. You read my worst times while changing, right? Maybe you don't want to go through that. I sure didn't but I had to. Think of it like getting a driver's license. You study, take a written exam, a driver's course, a driver's test, get a license, insurance and then, a car. Thank goodness there is a protocol for that. If you don't learn to drive, you will never get that shiny new car. And if you do get that car without going through the legal channels, you are setting yourself up for more problems in the long run.

Taking the cheater's route is never good. With that being said, I had to go through those awful moments so I could get to the other side. I had to weather the storm and, on most days, I really considered drowning over staying afloat. I had to prepare myself to let go of some things I believed I needed but no longer served me. As a matter of fact, all they did was try to keep me tethered to my problems.

Now here is one of the most rewarding things that happened after my graduation from fear. I freed up space in my spirit which was refilled by new and exciting desires and visions of being able to achieve my dreams!!! And the best part was that my husband had stood by me, even at the risk of his own happiness, and was happy to help me with my newly found awareness.

I have no doubt it was GOD who brought me those four simple words via another Spiritual soul knowing they were the keys to my inner freedom and my new Spiritual quest. Elements of surprise were those words of comfort. Bless him. Change me.

From this point on you have to decide where you want to go in your life and if you are willing to endure at all costs. Once you change you, you can then give elements of surprise to your partner who, if open, will receive them with total enthusiasm because you are no longer trying to force change. Spiritual changes are so smooth that your partner, if the right one for you, will go with the flow and start working on themselves without any coaxing. Yes I said if that partner is right for you.

Remember, I told you that when you begin to change, some things will have to go as they will no longer serve you. Yes, that can mean a spouse or family member and you can only get to where you are going when you release the non needed item. I am not advocating divorce but you have to know up front that truth cannot exist where there is a lie. If one of you gets to the heart of the matter and the other one doesn't want to face it then someone has to make a decision. Get my drift people?

On the flip side, your partner may be in awe with your changes and all of a sudden they, too, are doing things a little differently. Perhaps the two of you are able to communicate without screaming. Maybe you laugh more together. Maybe you will see why you should let your husband ride a motorcycle. Or tell your wife how gorgeous she is everyday. Now we are talking! The title for this chapter tells you that if you let me be me I will give you elements of surprise. Just so you are aware, when I said, "I will give you elements of surprise", I was not just referring to what you will introduce to your partner. I was letting you know about all the surprises you will give to yourself as well. Really, Rhayne? Really. Here is where you will be able to start exploring what you really love, desire, feel and need in order to get peaceful. This is so exciting I can't type fast enough to tell you about it!

Elements of self surprise (**aka: vicissitude**-unexpected changes, also in fortune). When you are out and about make mental notes about the things that gave your pleasure. When you get home make sure you jot them down on a piece of paper that you will see everyday. Pick one, close your eyes and imagine it. Feel it. Believe that it is yours to have. Some things will not be as easy to have immediately but you can always have them in a photo or in your mind. I live in the desert but I love the ocean so I think of it all the time. Here are some of the things you might want to explore to expand your thinking:

* What's your favorite season?
* Where is your dream vacation place?
* Do you like snow, rain, sunshine and/ or wind?
* What's your favorite scent?
* What new food would you like to try?
* Is there a hobby you would like to try?
* Do you have a favorite color?
* Is there a different hairstyle/color you want to try?
* Where would you like to live?
* Have you ever gone to a movie or restaurant alone?
* Are you affected by what others think?
* Are you happy with your body?
* Do you have positive friends?
* Is there a book you've been wanting to read?
* Have you ever had breakfast in bed?
* Have you ever touched a field of grass?

* Have you ever sent yourself flowers or a card?
* Have you ever looked in a mirror, naked, and told your body you loved it?

Those are just a few questions you can ask yourself to start the creative juices flowing. Please come up with your own questions because I am positive you have many that were hidden for years. Once you start answering your questions, be prepared to feel lighter, excited and full of ideas. You will start seeing easy ways to do the things you once thought were impossible. You will think of new ways to do old things. Your house looks a little drab? Grab a can of paint, a brush and voila! New rooms! Read home magazines. Look at cookbooks. Learn to use a drill. Take a bricklaying class. Questions are made to challenge your current thinking. Always keep in mind positive images you want to see unfold in your life and ignore any thoughts of what you cannot do. I am a pretty adventurous girl, as you already know, and some days I still surprise myself with new things I want to try. Now you are working on new things. Great. Let's go back to the animal kingdom and see how your new life may affect your partner and family members.

I want to talk about the octopus. I like them because they are smart mimics. Some years ago I watched a science show where there were two tanks and each one had an octopus in it. A twist top jar with a snail in it was dropped into tank B and that octopus was trying every way to open the jar. The other octopus was pressed up against his tank watching. The octopus eventually got tired and left the jar alone. Then a similar jar was dropped into tank A where that octopus already knew how to open the jar and octopus B watched every move. Octopus A opened the jar easily and got the snail treat. Octopus B was moving around in a frenzy once he saw the other one get the treat. The jar was dropped back into octopus B tank where it mimicked the same moves and easily opened the jar. Octopus A seemed excited once the other one learned the open move and both were swimming around in excitement. That is what the effect will be on those who surround you. Your newly found enthusiasm will be highly contagious which will continue to stoke your creative fires.

Spiritual freedom will allow you to eat the things you enjoy guilt free, go places alone to enjoy your own company and show you things you never knew you were good at no matter what anyone else says. We are winding down now. I know that makes you sad but there are a couple more chapters you may need to make sure your Spiritual journey keeps its focus.

THE DALAI HAS A L(L)AMA (AND OTHER MODES OF TRANSPORTATION)

I wish I came up with this chapter's title but the prize goes to Amy so all I'm going to do is expand on it. Or create it. Or make it up. Amy is a Spiritual prayer warrior. If there is a problem or need, get Amy to work her magical prayer powers and things start to move. I know that Amy's ability to pray people through their ordeals is her gift. The way she listens with her eyes tells people she can be trusted and she is really with them. Amy is like my own personal Dalai Lama. Who is Dolly Lima, Rhayne? Not Dolly Lima, Dalai Lama.

The Dalai Lama is a powerful Spiritual spokesperson for Tibet and Buddhism whose belief is consistent opposition to violence as recognized in 1989 with a Nobel Peace prize. In addition, The Dalai Lama has written books on both topics, speaks vastly about being able to eradicate violence and hatred through peace, harmony, patience and humility. The Dalai Lama is sometimes referred to as "His Holiness" and I am sure that is a title well earned. The word "Dalai" in Mongolian means "Ocean" and "Lama" is the equivalent of the Sanskrit word, "Guru". Together the title is "Ocean Teacher" meaning "teacher who is Spiritually as great as the ocean." Can you even wrap your mind around such a power? That is an all encompassing power meant for the good of all people and all things. All. Wow. To be Spiritually as great as the ocean sounds like a huge career choice but it, too, is a gift. And I have the nerve to think that my life is full of challenges!

Okay. We understand who the Dalai Lama is but what does he have to do with a llama? Being a play on words and having added so many other animals to my stories, the Dalai having a llama seemed like a perfect fit. The llama is a wild or domesticated South American cud chewing animal related to camels but smaller in size and lacking a hump. Poor thing. (Adult joke. Stay with me.) Llamas are animals that can be used for many purposes such as meat, dairy, wool, cart pulling and companionship, just to name a few. Being a llama is probably a hard job because, like the Dalai Lama, they take on many burdens for the good of others. Llamas can withstand high temperatures, long distances, heavy loads and the ultimate sacrifice of providing meat, all so others can have clothing, shelter, food and work. Not only is the llama all of the above, it is a smart animal which can be easily trained so it can be a pet for companionship. Can you understand why I thought the Dalai having a llama was a great idea? I now want you to find your own llama or other mode of Spiritual transportation.

It is said that the Dalai Lama meditates for hours per day for peace, centering and answers. I, like most of you, do not have hours to meditate, but I can give myself thirty minutes to one hour. Even fifteen minutes refreshes my mind and allows me to look at the day's situations with fresh eyes. Meditation is your gift to you. It will be your vehicle or mode of transportation to new ideas, undiscovered talents and inner peace with real tranquility.

I don't remember if I told you this before but meditation, for me, took and still takes, lots of discipline. I would rather do nine hundred other things than get still, which is what chaos wants you to do so fear can come back. Once I take ten minutes to sit and regroup, I am ready to receive through every channel of my life. Getting quiet so you can listen to the silence will unveil opportunities you would have missed in chaos. It will also help you sleep better, relax more easily and make you feel better overall.

Rhayne, how the heck do you know so much about the Dalai Lama and camels and whatnots? Glad you asked. I went to elementary school with him. Okay, that isn't true. The truth is, we meet for tea on Friday mornings. Okay, that isn't true either. But it is funny! Hahaha! Aren't I a riot!!

The real truth is, I read, observe, listen and do research. At the end of this book I will list many books that I believe will help you become more comfortable in finding your own way once my stories are over. Even if you don't read all of them, please read some of them for brain and spirit food. And don't make excuses about how you can't afford them, that's what the library is for.

Another mode of transportation to peace for me are creative outlets. My mind is so free when I am looking at the sky, painting a room, cooking a gourmet meal, watching a sunrise or set, curled up with a good book, volunteering my time to others or, just plain sitting and doing nothing. By the way, it has taken me forty years to learn how to do nothing and I still have to be cognizant while doing it so it doesn't feel like boredom. Over the last two years I have come to the conclusion that meditation is my mind's laxative. All the things I need are reviewed and kept and all the waste is eliminated so I can refuel. Yeah, yeah, I know…that isn't the most eloquent description but it is very clear to understand. Here are a few suggestions that might help you ease into peace:

* Find thirty minutes, once a week, to take a nap
* Go outside at night and just stare at the sky
* Handwrite a letter to a friend and mail it
* When you get home, don't turn on anything noisy for the first thirty minutes
* Breathe deeply and actually feel it
* Give yourself a facial
* Manually mow the lawn
* Stand in the rain and listen to it
* Throw your head back and laugh hard

* Buy a travel magazine & travel to each
  place in your mind with your eyes closed

* Slow roast an herb coated chicken and
  just smell the aroma while it bakes

There are billions of other ways to slow your mind but those are just some of my favorites because they work wonders for me. Besides, you never know where inspiration will come from when you aren't looking. I really do not want to leave this chapter because the next chapter is the final chapter and that always saddens me. But this time it also makes me happy knowing that you will be on your way to Spiritual freedom with a lifetime of peace and focus!

TRY IT DOGGIE STYLE!

Get your minds out of the gutter! I am talking about looking at your life from a different position. Sheesh! This is the last chapter therefore I want you to take all you can from it and know that I will be supporting your new journey through Spirit.

As you begin to broaden your new horizons you will experience all sorts of emotions because you have to go through to get through. Remember that from earlier? Do not give up or give in. Make sure you have a clear picture of what you want and where you want to go so when times get rough you can go back to that goal. Look at old problems from a different perspective.

If you've always opened your bills in a foul mood, try opening them when you feel good and tell yourself you are going to pay them with a smile. Weren't you smiling when the electric or gas company allowed you to have that account? If you are always driving out of control, try leaving a little earlier, cruising to your destination and enjoying the scenery. Take a different route. Take all the loose change in your pockets, purse or sofa, put it in a clear jar and label it with something you want. Maybe even start a holiday fund. Just a few more ideas:

* Wear a color you've never worn before
* Turn your phone off for one day and do not check messages
* Have spaghetti for breakfast
* Go to bed thirty minutes early
* Be thankful when you're handling your money, even if it's only a dime
* Buy a journal and write down all the good things that happen to you each day
* Try drinking more water everyday
* Try herbal teas

* Buy one small plant and watch it grow
* Listen to a different radio station
* Look through the classified ads
* Have a yard sale and make special plans for the proceeds
* Find something you're good at and become great at it
* Give openly and happily, *especially* when you don't think you can

So that is it. This journey with me is over. It is now your turn to go out into the world and continue to make it a better place by being a gentler soul. Get your children involved. Your enthusiasm will spill over and before you know it, you will be the life of the party, even if it is just your own party. I hope you have enjoyed this ride as it has been my pleasure sharing with you a part of me that, a few years ago, I didn't even know existed. And boy am I glad it does because it makes for a really wonderful gift that I can now pass on to you. GOD Bless & Safe Keeping!

LITTLE JEWELS I HAVE LEARNED FROM MY JOURNEY

* Where there is FAITH, there is NO fear

* What you believe, you attract

* People can change but only if **_they_** want to

* Love is unconditional

* Life is long and short

* I am worth loving

* All men do not cheat

* 10% to GOD, 10% to me, pay the IRS & the rest to that which keeps life comfortable

* Jealousy is ugly from a stranger but uglier from a loved one

* Chocolate milk really does come from brown cows

* Most religions have the same basic foundation

* If you give without attachments, you get so much more in return

* You are what you say you are

* It is what you say it is

* You are who you surround yourself with

* You are what you say others are

* Love is colorblind (Joan, Amy & Junne are living proof)

* Wherever you go, there you are

* Always make a joyful noise

* Some days you win, some days you win less

* When you're sure, be sure

* Nothing feels better than a two hour nap

* Worry and fear create mirages

* Enjoy where you are at this very moment

* Good mac&cheese is like a warm, fluffy blanket on a cold rainy day

* Smile no matter what they think

* Don't let the shade cover your sun

* Time is what you make it

* Vidalia onions are so yummy when caramelized

* My husband can be right, too

* Remove unhealthy elements from your world

* Some things you just have to let go in order to move forward

* The more you push, the harder it gets

* Animals don't gossip

* Animals aren't racists

* Just because someone's alive doesn't mean they are living

* If you take the road less traveled you will probably find me there

* Don't be at the airport when your ship comes in

* There is definitely a time to rest (thank you Pumpkin)

* Hens are just voluptuous chickens

* You can translate Don Quixote from Spanish to English if you have a year of patience

* Not everyone will be happy about your successes

* Not everyone wants to be a part of your successes

* Not everyone should be a part of your successes

* Rich people are regular people with money

* The comfort of a Tim Horton's double double coffee

* Inner anger takes away your power

* If Jimmy cracks corn, I don't care

* I like me. A lot

* Trust is necessary for growth

* Caterpillars are earthworms with expensive taste in coats

* **People _do_ judge a book by its cover!!!**

ACKNOWLEDGMENTS

GOD. As always, first. I thank you.

Proverbs 8:12 - I, wisdom, dwell with prudence, and find out knowledge of witty inventions.

My United States family:

My dad, my mom, my pumpkin, Carmen (cover queen), Amy (without you, no title), Anita (mi amiga para mi vida), Junne (keep your hands off fake flowers), Dario (for changing the MTA system), EARnest (thank you for fighting for our freedom), Bernie (always a retreat), Aegenis (hihowrya), Sonjay (SquareBiz!) Stephanie Dixon, Crystal in Mexico, Starr in Washington, Grunewald Guild, Music & Art class of 1984, Velanie, Rafe (real meditation), Melissa Service (CPCP), Murphi Johnson, Reyna & everyone at Glen Eden, AANR, Kim & everyone at DeAnza Springs, Tom & Mary of Terra Cotta Inn Resort, Wendy Dearborne, Carol Baker, Zorana with good hair, T-Roy, Mickki Brown, Milt & Madelyn, Pete V & the gang at BMW Motorcycles, Professor Monika, Ms Killeen & Mr Jerry, Dr. S. Dietz (O Solo Mio!), Cherie the Afghan Queen, Dr. Baxter, Dr. Wayne (cappuccino king), Florence & Doug, Linda & John, Gina (ultimate in strength), Heidi & Brenda & babies, Kim & Mark & Kali, Jaime & All of Sweet Monday, Joe Brown & Mama Brown, Christy, Waghi & Will, Delgado & his rhino bike, Olga & all my girls in Zumba & belly dance, Sadie, Roland & Atwater Villa, Henri at UPS and everyone else who has passed through my life making it more fun and valuable. I love you guys!

My Canadian Family

The entire Kurylo family including Sharon & Sylvia (I think we are even starting to look alike!), The Thompsons (food, fun & more of the same), Jim & Liz, Doug & Pat, Gail H, Charissa, Heidi & Unique Boutique, Donna Paisley, Chad & his talented staff at Pure Elements Spa, Tim Horton's coffee, Chapters Books,

Alberta Cross Cancer Institute, beautiful Sherwood Park and beautiful Edmonton Alberta. Thank you for EVERYTHING as there is way too much to mention. I love all of you forever!

My Indian Family

Quinn Habib Walker (come on, you had to know this was coming!), Ravi, Rosie, Carolyn, Nick & your lovely boys, Ali, Shahzad & your family, Smitta, Surinder and the rest of my family in Washington, Arizona, Oregon, Las Vegas and California. Thank you for embracing and teaching me about your culture, religion, food, tea (my absolute favorite!) and desserts. Your hospitality, prayers, well wishes and friendship are forever in my heart. I am truly honored to know all of you.

Those Who Are Nudging Me From Heaven

Aunt Julia, Aunt Rosetta, Cindy Berry, Cheryl Berry, Sallie Harrison, Keith Rossen, Steven Crossland, Rio, Annie, Ellie Mae & Schultz Thompson, Snickers Thomas and Godzilla Thomas. Not a day goes by that I don't think of you and how much joy each one of you brought to my life. I miss & love you.

Strangers Who Mattered

To everyone who has passed my way and brought a smile to my face on those days where I didn't think it was possible. Maybe at the bank, in the market or letting me in during a traffic merge. Thank you.

Rhayne's Research & Recommended Reading

The Bible — All Versions

Vinaya Pitaka

The Koran/Qur'an/Quran

The Richest Man in Babylon by George S. Clason

Quotes by Johann Wolfgang von Goethe

Quotes by Henry Ford

Eat, Pray & Love by Elizabeth Gilbert

Diary Of A Solitude by May Sarton

The Master Key by Charles F. Haanel

8 Steps to Create the Life You Want by Dr. Creflo A. Dollar Jr.

Books by Catherine Ponder:

* *The Dynamic Laws of Prosperity*

* *The Prosperity Secrets of the Ages*

* *Open Your Mind to Prosperity*

* *Open Your Mind to Receive*

Think and Grow Rich by Napoleon Hill

Webster's New World College Dictionary

Rhayne's Favorite Shows for Reference & Enjoyment Purposes & For Focus

The Golden Girls: four older roommates making the aging process & friendship fun

Judge Judy: a true New Yorker who gets right to the point

The Deadliest Catch: brave men facing the harshest conditions & still getting the job done

Dirty Jobs with Mike Rowe: people who do dirty jobs, with a smile, to make my life easier

House Hunters: seeing the endless possibilities of where & how I can live

The Barefoot Contessa with Ina Garten: because I loved the Shoppe when it was open

Everyday Italian with Giada De Laurentis: authentic Italian with a young, happy twist

Lidia's Italy with Lidia Bastianich: authentic Italian with old world charm

This Old House: so I can learn to restore my future dream Victorian

Lawrence Welk Show: allows me to reflect on simpler times

Sex & The City: four best friends in NYC with great fashions, great food & real situations

Dancing With the Stars: has me signing up for Argentine Tango lessons

New Scandinavian Cooking with Claus Meyer: keeps my goal of going to Norway alive

Sesame Street: the only show I've wanted to be on since 1968; imagination at its finest

Discovery Channel: increases my knowledge of the unknown

Animal Planet: makes all creatures smart and beautiful

As always,
feel free to email me to let me know
how your journey is coming along

Or

To tell me how much you enjoyed
my journey

Or

To tell me I'm the funniest
authoress you have ever had the
pleasure of meeting!

Reddeevahh@hotmail.com

www. rhaynethomas.com

Rhayne has struck again! Can you believe the hilarity of this title? But...don't let this title fool you as this jewel of a book is filled with personal stories that will allow you a rare look into the author's journey of her life. Filled with truth, pain and her usual quirky humor, she has opened her soul for the first time so that you, too, may find some light through your own window. A must read for anyone who needs to know that if life wasn't, isn't or hasn't been okay, it can certainly be okay through the powers of forgiveness, honesty, searching and, most of all, unconditional love. God Bless & Safe Keeping!

Made in the USA
Las Vegas, NV
28 January 2022